Northern Tuscany

Wolfgang Heitzmann
Renate Gabriel

Northern Tuscany

Florence – Appennine – Apuane Alps

Translated by Andrea Adelung

50 walks between Bologna and Florence,
Pisa and Carrara, Lucca and Abetone,
between the Riviera della Versilia and Casentino,
in the Appennine and in the Apuane Alps

With 122 colour photographs and one black and white picture,
49 walking maps in a scale of 1:50.000,
one city plan in a scale of 1:22.500 and
two overview maps in a scale of 1:600.000

ROTHER · MUNICH

Front cover:
The Castello della Verrucola near Fizzivano in Lunigiana

Frontispiece (photo on page 2):
Pizzo d'Uccello (left) and Monte Sagro (right) in the northern Apuane Alps

The photograph on Page 2 is by Mithra Omidvar, all other photos
within the book as well as on the cover are by the authors.

Cartography:
Walking maps © Bergverlag Rother GmbH, Munich
(drawn by Christian Rolle, Holzkirchen)

Translation
C. Ade Team (Andrea Adelung)

1st edition 2002
© Bergverlag Rother GmbH, Munich

ISBN 3-7633-4812-3

Distributed in Great Britain by Cordee, 3a De Montfort Street, Leicester
Great Britain LE1 7HD, www.cordee.co.uk
in USA by AlpenBooks, 3616 South Road, C-1, Mukilteo, WA 98275 USA,
www.alpenbooks.com

ROTHER WALKING GUIDES

Azores · Corsica · Côte d'Azur · Crete West · Cyprus · Gran Canaria · Iceland · La Palma ·
Madeira · Mallorca · Mont Blanc · Norway South · Provence · Sardinia · Sicily ·
High Tatra · Tenerife · Tuscany North · Valais East · Around the Zugspitze

**Dear mountain lovers! We would be happy to hear your opinion
and suggestions for amendment to this Rother walking guide.**

BERGVERLAG ROTHER · Munich
D-85521 Ottobrunn · Haidgraben 3 · Tel. (089) 608669-0, Fax -69
Internet www.rother.de · **E-mail** bergverlag@rother.de

Foreword

»This area is dominated by the horrible face of nature: a rocky mountain chain, a rubble pile of broken, torn elements, piles of astounding destruction...« No, you haven't picked up the wrong walking guide: That is exactly how Joseph Forsyth described La Verna, the sacred mountain in northeastern Tuscany, in the early 19th century, and his words would apply to several walking destinations between the Arno, the Appennine and the Apuane Alps.

The cliché of garden terrain – gentle hills with grapevines, olive and cypress trees – only applies to the area between Pisa and Florence, the cultivated land around the Monti Pisani, the Montalbano and the Pratomagno. Harshly beautiful, and not unlike the pre-Alps of Austria and Bavaria, on the other hand, are Mugello and Casentino, the northern provinces of Florence and Arezzo: Their mountain ridges, up to 1600m high, bear the largest and most beautiful forests of central Italy. To the west of them, in the mountain terrain of Pistoia, the peaks approach 1900m. Garfagnana, the »hinterland« of Lucca, seems very alpine in nature, as does Lunigiana, the northwestern tip of Tuscany, hardly known to tourists. The sandstone crests of the Appennine – partially due to their many gorges and lakes – are reminiscent of the eastern central Alps, while the Apuane Alps could very easily stand among the Dolomites. On clear days, from their sheer, jagged limestone and marble peaks, you can see as far as the nearby coast between Carrara and Viareggio: The Apuane Riviera and Versilia offer enjoyable bathing opportunities and a high-mountain experience all in one; just a few kilometres away from the sea, the marble quarries glisten in the sun like snow.

Our selection of walks not only focuses on the natural wonders, but of course also the rich cultural treasures of the region. In addition to the famous churches and monasteries, palaces and museums, villas and gardens, we were primarily interested in following the trail of everyday life: Crumbling walls remind us of the hard life in remote forests; some quarries had already been mined for Roman and Renaissance princes, and in countless mountain villages, the time seems to have stood still. Many of the walks presented here follow forgotten, partly roughly paved traffic connections, and two excursions even lead us back to the pioneer days of the railway.

We wish you pleasant holidays in northern Tuscany, exciting walks, and a healthy return!

Linz/Danube, Summer 2001   Wolfgang Heitzmann & Renate Gabriel

Contents

Tourist Information

Grade

Most of the walks presented in this guide lead through mountain terrain with summit elevations of between 1000 and 2000m, thus, through terrain comparable to the pre-Alps. The highest areas of the Appennine and parts of the Apuane Alps are high mountain ranges with steep escarpments and scree, sharp rocky ridges and walls of up to 700m high – several tours thus require good physical condition, sure-footedness and, in parts, also a head for heights. In order to be better able to assess the technical requirements of the walks, the numbers of the suggested routes are colour-coded as follows:

BLUE

These walks follow paths which are generally well-marked, sufficiently wide and only moderately steep, and thus can also be done with relatively little danger in poor weather. They are also suitable for older hikers as well as children.

RED

These routes have sections which are narrow and steep; they may be exposed over short sections. They should therefore only be undertaken by sure-footed mountain hikers.

BLACK

These routes are often narrow and have very steep passages. In places they are exposed; in some sections, scrambling is necessary. This means that these routes are only suitable for sure-footed, absolutely vertigo-free mountain climbers in good physical condition and with alpine experience. In the upper boundary of this tour category, there are climbing routes and ridge crossings having Difficulty Grade I and II, as well as secured climbing ascents which should only be attempted with the proper safety gear (chest and seat harnesses, rope and rope brakes and two fixed-rope krabs, helmet).

Access

International Airports: Galileo Galilei (Pisa); Amerigo Vespucci (Firenze).
Tuscany is accessible by train (London Waterloo Int. – Firenze S.M.N.; trains with sleeping or couchette cars, 18–19 hours).
When arriving by car, by the way, you do not necessarily have to travel the autostrada Bologna – Firenze: Between Liguria and Marche, 20 more or less well-developed mountain roads lead over the Appennine – e.g. over the Passo della Cisa, the Passo di Lagastrello, Abetone Pass, the Passo della Futa or over the Passo della Muraglione. All of these passes offer high-altitude starting points for walks which can be combined with a mountain hike.

Information

Great Britain: Italian State Tourism Board; 1, Princess Street; W1R 8AY London; tel 020/74081254, fax 74936695, e-mail enitlond@globalnet.co.uk
USA (New York): Italian Government Tourist Board; 630, Fifth Avenue - Suite 1565; New York, N.Y. 10111; tel 0212/2454822, fax 5869249, e-mail enitny@italiantourism.com
Canada: Office National Italie de Tourisme/Italian Government Travel Office; 175 Bloor Street East-Suite 907 - South Tower; Toronto (Ontario) M4W 3R8; tel 0416/9254882, fax 9254779, e-mail enit.canada@on.albn.com
Australia: Italian Government Tourist Office; Level 26, 44 Market Street; Sydney NSW 2000; tel 0292/621666, fax 621677, e-mail enitour@ihug.com.au
Internet: www.enit.it

Equipment

With the exception of a few walks near valleys, for which sneakers suffice, you should only undertake the walks in this guide with sturdy, ankle-high hiking shoes with non-slip soles. Furthermore, you will need sturdy, wind and rain-resistant clothing, a change of underwear, and, at higher altitudes, even in favourable weather, a sweater, hat and gloves. Your backpack should also contain provisions, a full litre or ½ litre water bottle and a small hiking first-aid kit. A sunscreen with a high SPF will protect you from the sun, as will a light cap or sunhat.

A feast by the lake: Picnic at Lago Baccio near Abetone in the Appennine.

Evening tranquillity on the beach of Viareggio. In the background the Apuane Alps.

Bathing

The 30-km long sandy beach of the Apuane Riviera and Versilia are among the most well-known and thus most frequented holiday regions in Italy. Between Marina di Carrara, Forte dei Marmi and Viareggio, there are up to 300m of wide beaches, which are divided into bagni over large stretches: In these consistently maintained sandy bathing beaches, bathing itself is free of charge, but one must rent the lounge chairs and umbrellas standing in long rows (the rate varies depending on season and bath). There are public access beaches between Marina di Massa and Forte dei Marmi, as well as south of the port of Viareggio. Several streams in mountain country offer more refreshing bathing opportunities than the sea. Water temperatures on the coast: May 17°C, June 21°C, July 23°C, August 24°C, September 23°C, October 20°C, November 18°C.

Train and bus

A few of the walks (especially those near larger cities) can be easily accessed by train and/or bus. From the main railway station in Florence, there are trains to Casentino (via Arezzo), Mugello (via Pontassieve), to Pisa (via Empoli), Viareggio (via Prato, Pistoia, Lucca) as well as to Bologna (via Prato). Other train lines: Pistoia – Bologna, Lucca – Aulla and La Spezia – Parma (via Aulla). Buses from Florence (bus terminal and several platforms next to the main train station!) to Abetone (COPIT), Bologna (SITA), Borgo San Lorenzo (SITA/CAP), Camaldoli and Chiusi La Verna (CAT/SITA), Lucca (Lazzi), Fiesole (city bus line 7), Montesenario (SITA), Padova (SITA), Pisa (Lazzi/SITA), Prato (CAP/Lazzi) or Vallombrosa (STIA), among other destinations. However, buses travel only infrequently, only on weekdays or not at all to more remote locations. In a few cases, access via bicycle or rental bicycle, mountain bike, or motor scooter is an alternative.

Note: bus tickets must be purchased before boarding in the offices of the bus terminal, in tobacco shops or bars, and railway tickets can be obtained in the train stations (when staff is on duty). Railway tickets must be validated before the trip. Buses are not always on time; by the way, they not only sometimes leave too late, but may also leave a few minutes too early! You can obtain bus schedules e.g. at the bus terminal in Florence (right next to the railway station), and train schedules at newsstands. Taxis are somewhat cheaper than they are north of the Alps; however, several surcharges are levied (agree on a price in advance for cross-country trips).

Camping

There are over 200 camping grounds in all of Tuscany, most of which, however, are located in the coastal regions and on the island of Elba. The national tourist office ENIT publishes a new directory every year of all camping grounds, holiday villages and youth hostels (see Information); the ADAC camping guide for Southern Europe also offers a good overview.

Food and accommodation

All food and accommodation opportunities along the route are indicated for each tour description. The huts of the Club Alpino Italiano (CAI) in the Appennine and Apuane Alps are smaller and simpler than those in the Alps, but very cosy and well-maintained. Opening times can vary, especially outside of the summer months, depending on weather and snow conditions. Those wishing to stay overnight should definitely make reservations in advance.

Optimal accommodations for walking holidays are offered by Agroturismo, the Italian version of »Holiday on the Farm.« Several farms offering rooms or holiday flats with and without board are situated in the beautiful countryside. You can obtain addresses from the local tourist offices.

A portion of this walking guide was written at Prà di Reto, the cosy farm

Marble kitchen in the Rif. Conti (Walk 44).

of our friends, Olinto and Alessandra Punti, in the medieval village of Gragnanella, above Castelnuovo Garfagnana (tel/fax 0583/65734, e-mail pradireto@hotmail.com).

Holidays

Natale, Santo Stefano (25th/26th December), Capodanno (1st January), Epifania (6th January), Pasqua (Easter Sunday and Monday), Anniversario della Liberazione (anniversary of the liberation from the German army on 25th April), 1st May, Fondazione della Repubblica (anniversary of the founding of the Republic on the first Sunday in June), Ferragosto (15th August – on this day, all of Italy is underway), Ognissanti (1st November) and Festa dell'Immacolata (8th December).

In addition, practically every town and village celebrates local festivals with religious roots, or with historical competitions (information available at the tourist offices).

Dangers

It can be very difficult to find one's orientation in fog. Especially on the west side of the Apuane Alps, facing the sea, clouds develop early in the day, even in beautiful, sunny weather – thus, start your walk early. Do not

Caution in quarries!

underestimate thunderstorms and sudden downpours, which can turn even dry gullies into wild streams within minutes. Sudden flood waves have destroyed entire villages. The only defence: Turn back before it is too late! Individual stretches of path can often be damaged or blocked off by landslides.

Falling rock is a hazard under rock walls and around quarries – especially the marble quarries of the Apuane Alps, over whose scree giant boulders roll downward.

You do not have to be afraid of wild animals, but pay attention to suspicious rustling in the grass: the Aspis viper (up to 75 cm long with black rings on grey, light or reddish-brown background, yellow tail tip and wide, triangular head) is more poisonous than the adder. Thus: do not go walking in sandals, and, before sitting down on grass, hit the area with a stick several times.

In the winter, the mountains of Tuscany are also covered in snow. The high humidity often leads to icing; northern cirques can be covered in hard, old snow right up into June.
Emergency number: tel 113 (police)

Walking times

The walking times indicated are average, not guaranteed values, and only include the pure walking time without rests or photography breaks. The walking times indicated in Italian guides or on signs were evidently determined by well-trained *alpinisti* – more leisurely walkers should add up to 25% to those times.

Maps and markers

The best overview maps: Kümmerly & Frey »Tuscany« on a scale of 1:200,000.

On a scale of 1: 50,000, there is the Kompass Hiking Map 646 »Alpi Apuane – Garfagnana – Carrara – Viareggio«. Hiking maps with a great deal of detail on selected areas (Montalbano, Pratomagno, Parco Nazionale delle Foreste Casentinesi) are available from S.E.L.C.A. Firenze on a scale of 1:25,000. The maps of Edizioni Multigraphic on a scale of 1:25,000 are also useful, which are based on military maps and are available in editions having two pages each (printed on the front and back) of all mountain areas in northern Tuscany – in Florence, for example, at Feltrinelli (Via dei Cerretani, 33r) or Il Viaggio (Borgo degli Albizzi, 41r), in other towns usually at the APT tourist office, in tobacco shops and even in some supermarkets. In Great Britain, they are available at Cordee, 3a De Montfort Street, LE1 7HD Leicester, www.cordee.co.uk (tel 0116/2543579).

Almost all of the routes presented here are more or less well marked (the Club Alpino Italiano (CAI) usually uses red and white markers, as in the Alps).

Climbing

There are climbing opportunities in all mountain areas, especially in the Apuane Alps, but also in various cliffs of the Apennine submountains (e.g. in Monsummano Terme). Climbing courses are offered in Garfagnana (information in the Castelnuovo Garfagnana tourist office), among other places.

Fixed rope routes

In the Apuane Alps, there are five fixed rope routes which should only be used with the appropriate equipment (helmet, chest and seat harness, ropes with rope brakes and two fixed-rope krabs): the Via Ferrata del Procinto above Stazzema (Walk 48), Via Ferrata Salvadori on Monte Forato (Walk 47), Via Ferrata Vecchiacchi straight across the eastern flank of Monte Sella, as well as three routes on Pizzo d'Uccello, Via Ferrata di Foce

Siggioli on Pizzo d'Uccello (Walk 37), Via Ferrata Piotti from Vinca to Foce di Giovo and Via Ferrata Zaccagna from Equi Terme to Cresta Nattapiana. Furthermore, there are short secured passages, e.g. in the area of the Rifugio Nello (Walk 44) south of Campocatino (Walk 34), but also at Libro Aperto (Walk 23) or on Monte Giovo (Walk 25) in the Appennine.

Fixed rope route to Foce Siggioli (W. 37).

Climate and hiking season

The best times for walks are the spring, the late summer and early autumn. In summer, you should start out very early in the day. The late autumn and winter bring unpredictable weather conditions, but always a few beautiful days in between for walking in the lower areas. The most precipitation falls between October and December, and then again in March and April.

Average daily high temperatures in Florence:

Month	1	2	3	4	5	6	7	8	9	10	11	12
°C	8.3	10.0	14.0	18.5	22.8	27.9	30.9	29.9	25.5	19.0	13.3	9.1

Mountain biking

The Tuscan mountains provide ideal terrain for mountain-bikers: Hundreds of kilometres of isolated forestry roads cross the forest slopes of the Appennine and the middle elevations of the Apuane Alps; manoeuvrable paths even reach mountain ridges in several spots. Several of the walks presented here can be expanded into »bike & hike« tours. A few Italian bike guides, such as »Apuane sui pedali« (Pezzini Editore, Viareggio) can provide inspiration for such tours.

Opening times

Most shops open from Monday to Friday at 8:30 or 9:00 a.m., and close for a midday break between 12:30 or 1:00 p.m. until 3:00 or 3:30 p.m. and close at 7:30 p.m. (in summer, they often do not open again until 4 or 5 p.m. and close at 8 or 8:30 p.m.).On Saturday afternoon and Sunday, the shops remain closed, except for those in tourist centres; some grocery stores, however, are open on Sunday morning. You can generally visit churches from 7 to 12 or 1 p.m. daily, and between 4 or 5 p.m. and 7 or 8 p.m. – please do not walk through the church during mass! Opening times for museums vary everywhere; they even change several times throughout the year. State museums are closed on Monday (information available at the tourist offices).

Paragliding

You can go paragliding in San Marcello Pistoiese or in Abetone, for instance. For information call Toscana Parapente, tel. 0573/622408.

Cycling

Second only to soccer, it is the national sport in Italy! There are only a few developed bicycle paths, but many side streets with little traffic invite cyclers for a pleasant, leisurely ride (Italian drivers are usually very considerate of people on bicycles; some sound their horns before overtaking). The mountain roads and passes in the Appennine and Apuane Alps are among the greatest challenges for athletic cyclists.

Telephone

The country code when dialling to Italy is 0039; the 0 in the subsequent area code may not be omitted – just as when phoning within Italy. From Italy to Great Britain, dial 0044, to Ireland 00353, to USA/Canada 001, to Australia 0061, to New Zealand 0064, then omit the subsequent 0 of the area code. It is much cheaper to phone from SIP phone boxes than from hotels or via mobile phone; the telephone cards needed can be purchased in tobacco shops and bars – do not forget to tear off the perforated corner before using!

Trekking

Long-distance hiking – »trekking« – is becoming more and more popular in Toscana, too. Almost every province has its own long-distance hiking route: Casentino Trekking (CT), Sorgenti di Firenze Trekking (SOFT, circumnavigating Mugello, with 22 alternatives), Montagna Pistoiese Trekking (MPT), Valleriana Trekking (VT, north of Pescia), Garfagnana Trekking (GT) or Trekking Lunigiana (TL, circuit trail at an intermediate altitude). The difficult circuit through the Apuane Alps and the Grande Escursione Appenninica (GEA, 1400km), a part of the European Long-Distance Hiking Route E 1, is only recommended for experienced hikers. The huts and simple accommodations (Posti Tappa) in the destination towns of each leg serve as bases.

Winter sport

North of the Alps, Tuscany is not exactly a Mecca for skiers, but, those who are nevertheless looking for fun on the slopes will find it in Abetone, among other locations. When the snow and avalanche conditions are favourable, ski tours can even be undertaken in the Appennine and Apuane Alps; the more gentle forest mountains can also be traversed with terrain-appropriate cross-country skis or snowshoes.

Starting Points and Excursion Destinations

Abetone Apennine crossing (1388m) between Pistoia or Lucca and Modena, today, the largest Italian winter sport town outside of the Alps. Both border pyramids (1777) are worth seeing, as is the botanical forest garden near Sestaione valley. Tel. 0573/60231.

Arni Small marble-quarry village in the wild, rocky terrain of the central Apuane Alps; access from Castelnuovo Garfagnana and on an impressive mountain road from Massa. In a difficult-to-reach gorge at the foot of the southern face of Monte Sumbra, the Marmite dei Giganti are hidden (large whirlpool holes carved out of the brook bed by large stones being whirled around).

Artimino Fortified village above Arno valley between Florence and Empoli. Romanesque church outside of the village, Etruscan museum in Villa Medicea La Ferdinanda (Villa Artimino), the »Villa with the hundred chimneys«.

Aulla The capital and traffic hub of the Lunigiana was almost completely destroyed in World War II. On a hill overlooking the town stands the Fortezza della Brunella (Museo di Storia Naturale della Lunigiana with a nature reserve). Excursion destinations in the vicinity: Castello di Malgrate and Museo Etnografico della Lunigiana in Villafranca in Lunigiana (12km to the north), Castello di Terrarossa in Licciana Nardi (10km to the northeast), castle ruins of Tresana (8km to the northwest).

Badia di Moscheta A secluded monastery situated in the expansive woods between Mugello and Firenzuola dating from the 11th century; Museo del Paesaggio Serena dell'Appennino.

Bagni di Lucca Once world-famous, today a tranquil spa town (thermal springs with iron content) with villas, parks and an impressive chain bridge north of Lucca, near the confluence of the Lima and Serchio. Near Borgo a Mozzano, approx. 3km to the south, the famed Ponte della Maddalena (Ponte del Diavolo) spans the Serchio with five arches of varying sizes.

Bagnone Small city with an old castle in central Lunigiana, situated in the panoramic submountains of the Appennine. The castle ruins of Treschietto can be found 2.5km to the northeast.

Barga Fortified town high above the central Serchio valley with a magnificent view of the Apuane Alps, rising up opposite the town. The Duomo San Cristofano (11th century, interesting marble pulpit) reigns above the medieval centre of town, the Palazzo Pancrazi, the Bar Capretz and the Teatro dei Differenti. See Walk 28.

Bibbiena   Capital of Casentino. An attractive old part of town around the Pieve di Santi Hippolito e Donato (12th century) and the Palazzo Dovizi (with a theatre). Museo Archeologico in Partina (6km northeast of town).

Bivigliano   Small climatic health resort north of Florence, at the foot of the monastery mountain Monte Senario. Cultural events are often held in the Villa di Bivigliano, located somewhat outside of town.

Borgo San Lorenzo   Capital of Mugello, 25km north of Florence. The Palazzo del Podestà, the church with the hexagonal tower and the Villa Pecori Giraldi (with its Museo Chini and Park) are worth seeing. **i** Via Togliatti 45, tel. 055/8495346.

Calci   Small town east of Pisa, at the foot of the Monti Pisani. The Certosa di Calci, established in 1366, (also known as Certosa di Pisa), which in the 17th century was decorated sumptuously, is located outside of town (Museo di Storia Naturale del Territorio).

Camaiore   Peaceful little town in a valley basin beneath the southern foothills of the Apuane Alps, in the vicinity of Badia San Pietro, which dates back to the 7th century, and 10km away from the beach resort of Lido di Camaiore.

Camaldoli   Permanent monastery of the Monk Hermits of Camaldoli, established in the year 1046, 814m high in the wooded mountains in the north of Casentino. The monastery apothecary from the 16th century and the Museo Forestale are noteworthy. Six km further up is the hermitage of the same name (1012) – each monk lived in his own little house.

Cantagallo   A mountain village in the north of Prato in the spring area of the Fiume Bisenzio. Centro per l'Educazione Ambientale di Cave.

Carrara   World-famous marble city (60 000 inhabitants) near the sea on the western slope of the

The snow-white marble quarries above Torano, a part of Carrara.

17

Apuane Alps, along with Massa, the capital of the province of Lunigiana. Cathedral (11th century), Fonte del Gigante, Museo Civico del Marmo, Accademia di Belle Arti. The ride to the nearby villages of Torano, Frantiscritti (small museum marble quarry) and Colonnata offer breathtaking scenery: They are surrounded by 300 marble quarries, some reaching up to the mountain peaks. **i** in Marina di Carrara, tel. 0585/632218.

Carregine   Medieval mountain village at the foot of Monte Sumbra in the Apuane Alps; access from Poggio in the Garfagnana. There are several shepherd's huts with stone-covered roofs in the surrounding area.

Casola Lunigiana   This attractive mountain village in the north of the Apuane Alps houses the interesting Museo del Territorio. On the Colle Argenga, 1034m, over the Passo Carpinelli, the nearby crossing from Garfagnana to Lunigiana, is the pilgrimage church with the Madonna della Guardina (and a beautiful view of the Apuane Alps).

Castagno d'Andrea   Summer holiday spot in the east of Mugello, on the slope of Monte Falterona. Birthplace of the early Renaissance painter Andrea del Castagno. Access from San Godezo (Romanesque pillar basilica).

Castelnuovo Garfagnana   Capital and traffic hub of Garfagnana, hiking centre. The Fortezza di Monte Alfonso towers above the city (pretty, short walk on Sentiero dell'Ariosto), in the centre of town, the Rocca Ariostesca (where the Renaissance poet Ludovico Ariosto once lived, author of the Orlando Furioso; Museo del Territorio). Information Piazza delle Erbe, tel. 0583/65169.

Castelnuovo Magra   Old little town with a castle on a hill northwest of Carrara, which is located in Liguria.

Castiglione Garfagnana   Mountain town surrounded by a wall ring above Castelnuovo Garfagnana, situated on the road to Radici Pass. The old hospice San Pellegrino in Alpe (Museo Etnografico Provinciale) is located 11km above the town (south of the pass) .

Chiusi della Verna   Once a fortified pass, today a summer holiday destination at the crossing from Casentino to the upper Tiber valley. The noteworthy monastery La Verna (Chiesa Maggiore, grottos and museum), dating back to Saint Francis, is located on the craggy Sasso Nudo above the city. Caprese Michelangelo, the birthplace of Michelangelo Buonarroti (1475 – 1564), is situated 10km to the southeast.

Cirone   Small mountain village beneath the pass of the same name between Parma and Pontremoli in the upper Lunigiana (situated on the northern side of the Apennines in Emilia-Romagna). Entrance to the »Nature Reserve of the Hundred Lakes«.

Collodi The picturesque village built up along the steep hill between Pescia and Lucca is the birthplace of Carlo Lorenzini (Collodi), the author of *Pinocchio*. The Giardino Garzoni, located beneath the village, is a prime example of baroque gardening art, with stairs, waterworks and a maze, and the neighbouring, originally-designed Parco di Pinocchio attracts not only small guests.

Corfino Mountain village on the heavily-wooded southwestern side of Garfagnana, divided by gorges; access from Castelnuovo. In the nature reserve Orecchiella, located above the village, one can see traditional, thatched huts; the most popular excursion destinations are the visitor centre, the bear preserve, a 25-minute walk from the visitor centre, and the beautifully-situated Orto Botanico at the foot of the rocky Pania di Corfino.

A success story with a long nose: Pinocchio has become a symbol for Collodi.

Coreglia Antelminelli This very photogenic village lies just west of Barga on the slope of the Appennine, high above the central Serchio valley. A museum displays several plaster figures (figure di gesso), which were once sold by emigrants throughout Europe.

Cutigliano Attractive mountain town in the Appennine above Lima valley, south of Abetone. Eye-catchers include the Chiesa San Bartolomeo and the Palazzo dei Capitani della Montagna, decorated with a coat-of-arms. Museo della gente dell'Appennino Pistoiese in Rivoreta (9km to the northwest). **i** tel. 0573/68029.

Equi Terme This friendly spa town in the south of Lunigiana has a medieval town centre at Fosso di Fagli, directly under the rock walls of the Apuane Alps. The neighbouring town of Monzone, built on a precipitous rock, is also worth seeing.

Fabbriche di Vallico This mountain village in a tributary valley of Serchio in the southern Apuane Alps was once established by blacksmiths from

Bergamo (access between Borgo a Mozzano and Gallicano). In the expansive woods around the village, you can find several original villages and the traditional huts used to roast and store chestnuts.

Fiesole   Pretty little town (15 000 inhabitants) on a hill in the north of Florence. Interesting sights include the Etruscan-Roman excavation sites, including a well-preserved theatre (2500 seats) and an archaeological museum, the Duomo San Romolo (11th cent.), the Bandini Museum, the Costantini antique collection and the Franciscan monastery (with museum). Beneath the village is the beautifully-decorated Badia Fiesolana. **i** at Piazza Mercato, tel. 055/598720.

Firenze (Florence)   The capital of the region of Tuscany (375 000 inhabitants) and »world art capital« is visited by about 2.6 million tourists each year. The highlights of the city's centre: octagonal baptistery (believed to date from the 4th cent., with green and white marble decoration, mosaics in the dome and a great bronze portal) in Piazza di San Giovanni in front of the Duomo Santa Maria del Fiore (construction began in 1296) with its 84.7-m high Campanile and 114.4-m high dome by Filippo Brunelleschi (1377 – 1446), Loggia del Bigallo, Museo dell'Opera del Duomo, Palazzo del Bargello (collection of sculptures), Badia Fiorentina, Casa di Dante, Casa Buonarroti, Franciscan church Santa Croce (with the graves of Michelangelo, Galileod, Machiavelli), Museo di Storia della Scienza, Piazza della Signora with a number of sculptures (including a copy of the famous David by Michelangelo, the Neptune fountain by Ammannati and the sculpture »Rape of the Sabine Women«), the Palazzo Vecchio (city hall) with its 94-m high tower, and next to it the Galleria degli Uffizi (one of the most famous painting galleries in the world, e.g. containing the »Birth of Venus« by Botticelli), San Lorenzo (parish church of the Medici), Santo Spirito, Galleria

The Campanile of the Palazzo Vecchio, as seen from Giardino di Boboli.

Landmark of the capital city: The 85-m high Campanile and the massive dome of the Duomo Santa Maria del Fiore, 6m higher.

dell'Accademia (with the original David Michelangelo), the San Marco monastery and Mercato Centrale. The botanical gardens and several beautiful parks offer relaxation in a green environment. South of the Arno (Oltrarno): the monumental Palazzo Pitti (16th cent) with its expansive Giardino di Boboli, Capella Brancacci (Frescoes). The Arno is spanned by the Ponte Vecchio, characterized by its superstructure (containing several goldsmith shops and the Corridoio Vasariano, a secret passageway connecting the Uffizi with the Palazzo Pitti). To the southeast, on a hill overlooking Piazzale Michelangelo (with a beautiful view of the city), sits the San Miniato al Monte church, with its magnificent marble façade. **i** Via Manzoni 16, tel. 055/23320; Chiasso Baroncelli 17/19 (in front of the main train station), tel. 055/212245.

Firenzuola This town, established on the northern slope of the Appennine as early as the 14th cent. in the »Romagna Toscana« in the north of the province of Florence, was badly damaged in World War II. Today, it is a centre of sandstone mining (for more information: Museo della Pietra Serena).

Fivizzano The »Florence of the Lunigiana« is situated above the Torrente Rosaro, between Aulla and the Passo del Cerreto in the Appennine. Noteworthy: the Palazzo dell'Arcade Labindo, the baroque fountain, and, above all, the angular Castello della Verrucola.

Forte dei Marmi Once a fortification and marble loading station in Versilia, today a popular spa. **i** Via Achille Franceschi 8/b, tel. 0584/80091.

Fosdinovo The most attractive castle in Lunigiana, situated in the north-western Apuane Alps near Sarzana on the Ligurian border.

Gallicano Situated beneath Barga in the central Serchio valley. The town is the starting point for a special attraction of the Apuane Alps: The Grotta del Vento near Fornovolasco in the rear-most portion of Turrite valley is one of the largest cave systems in Italy, and contains fascinating underground streams and colourful stalactite and stalagmite decorations (three guided tours lasting between 1 and 3 hrs.). On the way to the wind cave, the access road and a walking path also branch off to Eremo di Calomini: The monastery is »stuck« under an overhanging rock wall.

Gramolazzo This summer holiday destination lies on a reservoir beneath the highest peak in the Apuane Alps, the Monte Pisano; access from Piazza al Serchio in upper Garfagnana. On the other side of a tunnel, one can access the picturesque village of Minucciano.

Isola Santa An abandoned mountain village on a reservoir in the valley of Turrite Seccaon on the adventurous road leading from Castelnuovo Garfagnana through the Apuane Alps to Massa.

Levigliani Old quarry village at the foot of Monte Corchia in the southern Apuane Alps: access from Seravezza in Versilia.

The Duomo San Martino in Lucca.

Lucca The medieval province capital (86 000 inhabitants) between Pisa and the Apuane Alps is surrounded by a completely preserved circular city wall. Noteworthy: Duomo San Martino with its splendid marble façade, Museo della Cattedrale, Chiesa San Frediano, Chiesa San Michele, Piazza Anfiteatro, Palazzo Mansi (with the Pinacoteca Nazionale), Palazzo Pfanner (with a beautiful garden), the birth house of Giacomo Puccini, Museo della città (interactive museum in the interior of Baluardo San Paolino), botanical garden. **i** at the Piazzale Verdi, tel. 0583/419689.

Famous villas and parks in the environs: Villa Reale in Marlia, Villa Grabau and Villa Oliva in San Pancrazio, Villa Mansi in Segromigno in Monte, Villa in Camigliano (all locations 7 to 10km northeast of the city), Villa Bernardini in Vicopelago (5km to the south).

Massa   Close to the sea on the western slope of the Apuane Alps, and, together with Carrara a province capital of Lunigiana (68 000 inhabitants). Castello Malaspina towers above Piazza Aranci in the centre; the square itself is dominated by Palazzo Cybo Malaspina. Worthwhile excursions include the Castello Aghinolfi in Montignoso (4km to the southeast) and the Orto Botanico »Pietro Pellegrini« in the Apuane Alps (16km on the mountain road in the direction of Castelnuovo di Garfagnana, near the Rifugio Città del Massa; guided tours only).

Massaciuccoli   Village northeast and above the lake of the same name between Viareggio and Lucca. Noteworthy sites include the Roman excavation finds, a Roman villa with thermal baths near the church, and the small natural-history museum in the Oasi of the bird-protection organization LIPU.

Monsummano Terme   Spa town between Pistoia and Lucca, on the edge of Montalbano. Worth seeing: Museo della Città e del Territorio, Grotta Giusti and Grotta Parlanti thermal baths, fortified village of Monsummano Alto (11th cent.). i Piazza IV Novembre 1, tel. 0572/9590.

The Romanesque church on the hill of Monsummano Alto.

Montecatini Terme   The ostentatious spa town 5km west of Monsummano was among the most frequented travel destinations in Europe in the 19th century. It offers fancifully-designed thermal baths, contemporary art in the Pinacoteca Dino Scalabrino as well as a cog railway up to the high-altitude village of Montecatini Alto (castle). i Viale Verdi 66, tel. 0572/772244.

Palazzuolo sul Senio A town in »Romagna Toscana«, east of Firenzuola. The Palazzo del Capitano houses the Museo della Vita e del Lavoro delle Genti di Montagna; the neighbouring town of Marradi is the home of the baroque Badia del Borgo.

Passo della Futa 903-m high Apennine crossing between Bologna and Florence. The Cimitero di Guerra Germanico, the largest soldier's cemetery in Italy, is the last resting place of 30 683 fallen.

The hamlet of Monte a Pescia high above Valdinievole.

Pescia This lovely city is situated on both sides of the river of the same name, and has two city centres, around the Chiesa San Francesco and in Piazza Mazzini. Pescia is considered the largest European flower market in Europe outside of Holland, and possesses a large flower exchange. Other noteworthy sites: the Gipsotheka Libero Andreotti in the Palazzo della Podestà, old paper factories in Pietrabuona, located to the north, the wine town of Montecarlo (5km to the southwest) and the ten »castle villages« on the little-known, chestnut-wooded hills of Svizzera Pesciatina – from Vellano to Pontito.

Pietrasanta This pretty capital of Versilia (25 000 inhabitants) is situated beneath the precipitous southern craggy precipice of Monte Altissimo; it is considered the centre of industrial processing and artistic refinement of marble. Eye-catchers include the Duomo San Martino, with its brick-red Campanile, several Palazzi, the archaeological museum, the Museo dei Bozzetti (marble sculptures) and several marble studios. Above the town, the mountain village of Sant'Anna di Stazzema is a reminder of unimaginable slaughter: In August of 1944, German troops murdered 560 men, women and children here – the youngest victim was 20 days old.

Pievepelago A summer resort in the north of Abetone, located in Emilia-Romagna. Starting point to the Parco dell'Alto Appennino Modenese and for the walks around Lago Santo Modenese.

Pisa The university city and province capital (97000 inhabitants) was located on the sea during the Roman age; today, it is situated 12km away from the mouth of the Arno river. The world-famous Leaning Tower is located in the Piazza dei Miracoli. Less known are the other »miracles«: the Duomo Santa Maria Assunta (with its museum), the baptistery (the largest baptistery in the world) and the cemetery Camposanto (with soil from Jerusalem); across from it is the Museo delle Sinopie (red chalk drawings as fresco sketches). Noteworthy sites in the centre of town: the churches Santa Maria della Spina and San Paolo a Ripa d'Arno, Museo dell'Opera del Duomo, Museo Nazionale di San Matteo, Museo Virtuale, the oldest botanical gardens in the world, and Keith Haring's Comic figure in Piazza San Antonio. **i** Via Cammeo 2, tel. 050/560464.

Pistoia The bustling province capital (87 000 inhabitants) northwest of Florence is proud of its historical centre, which houses several Gothic and Renaissance buildings. Special sights: Duomo San Zeno e Jacopo (with its beautiful silver altar), Museo di San Zeno, Capella del Tau, Museo Civico, Itinerario del Ghiaccio (old ice cellar). The Giardino Zoologico is situated 4-km west of the city. **i** at the Piazza del Duomo tel. 0573/21622.

Undiscovered Tuscany: the magical old town of Pontremoli in Lunigiana.

Pontremoli The historical centre of upper Lunigiana was established on the ancient Franconian road along which the German emperors advanced to Rome. The pretty old town around the cathedral, with its large dome and the Castello del Piagnaro (interesting Museo delle Statue-Stele dedicated to historic statues) are worth seeing. Centro Malaspina in Mulazzo, 10km away, in whose vicinity is also the Castello di Lusuolo.

Poppi Medieval village in Casentino, near Bibbiena. The Castello dei Conte Guidi, before which stands a bust of Dante Alighieri, is one of the best-preserved castles in Tuscany; in the vicinity, animal lovers can visit the Fauna Europa zoo. Museo della Castagna in Raggiolo (9km southwest of town).

Prácchia   A former thermal bath north of Pistoia, at the northern portal of the Apennine tunnel of Porrettana, the first railway line between Bologna and Tuscany.

Prato   This province capital (170 000 inhabitants), located only 16km northwest of Florence, is known as the centre of the Italian textile industry. It possesses a remarkable medieval old town around the Castello dell'Imperatore (Hohenstaufen castle), the Duomo Santo Stefano (with its famous exterior pulpit), the Museo dell'Opera del Duomo, the Museo Civico and the Museo del Tessuto (textile museum). The Museo d'Arte Contemporanea, a centre for contemporary art, rare for Italy, is located close to the motorway exit Prato Est. Excursion destinations in the south of the city: Villa Medicea in Poggio a Caiano, Villa Montalvo in Campi Bisenzio, Museo del Design in Quarrata. **i** Via Cairoli 48, tel. 0574/24112.

Pratovecchio   Town in upper Casentino, seat of the Parco Nazionale delle Foreste Casentinesi. The Romanesque church of Romena and the Castello di Romena (Dante was a guest here; museum, guided tours only) are located to the west above the town. Castello di Palagio and Collezione d'Arte Contemporanea in the neighbouring village of Stia.

Resceto   The former quarry village in a remote and rocky valley end in the northern Apuane Alps; access from Massa.

Rufina   Wine-growing town in eastern Mugello, in the smallest of the seven Chianti wine regions. Wine fans can visit the Museo delle Vite e del Vino in the villa Medicea di Poggio Reale.

Sambuca Pistoiese   One of several original mountain villages on the northern slope of the Appennine above Limentra di Sambuca, north of the Passo della Collina at the connection of Bologna – Pistoia. Itinerario della Pietra in Pavana.

San Benedetto in Alpe   The small mountain village is situated below the Passo del Muraglione on the mountain torrent Acqua Cheta, just north of the border to Emilia-Romagna.

San Marcello Pistoiese   Summer holiday resort amid the thick woods between Pistoia and Abetone, main town of Pistoiese mountain country. Worthwhile walks: Itinerario del Ferro and Itinerario dell'Arte Sacra e Religiosità Popolare in the neighbouring town of Popiglio, in whose vicinity the spectacular Ponte Sospeso (suspension bridge) is located, which spans the Lima. **i** Via Marconi 16, tel. 0573/630145.

San Mommè (Sammommè)   Small summer resort in the mountain country of Pistoia, at the southern portal of the Apennine tunnel of Porrettana, whose curvy and tunnel-rich southern ramp is one of the most beautiful railway lines in Italy.

San Piero a Sieve   Fort San Martino stands watch above the small traffic hub in Mugello, located beneath the large Sieve reservoir. A few castle-like villas of the Medici's' are located in the vicinity, such as the Castello del Trebbio.

Sarzana   This city, surrounded by a wall, is situated northwest of Carrara, near the mouth of the Magra flowing into the sea, and thus in Liguria. Noteworthy are the Duomo Santa Maria Assunta and the Pisani Citadella. In the vicinity, you can find the remains of the mighty Roman city of Luni, which takes its name from the neighbouring Lunigiana (large excavation site with a very interesting museum).

Sassalbo   The small summer holiday resort on the Passo del Cerreto, the crossing from Reggio nell'Emilia to Lunigiana, is one of a series of original mountain villages beneath the wild Apennine peaks of Lunigiana: Serravalle, Rocca Sigillina, Vignolo di Lusignana, Treschietto, Compione, Apella, Tavernelle, Comano, Camporaghena, Torsana.

Scarperia   Fortified little town at the connection from Mugello to Firenzuola. The Palazzo dei Vicari resembles a miniature Palazzo Vecchio in Florence, the Museo dei Ferri Taglienti provides information on the local saw and cutting-tool makers. Museo di Casa d'Erci in Grezzano to the east of the town.

Seravezza   Centre of marble mining in Versilia. In the Museo del Lavoroe delle Tradizioni Popolare, you can find out a great deal about the work of the marble cutters. Excursion tip: Pieve alla Capella on the road to Azzano, at the foot of Monte Altissimo (the window rosette is considered the »eye of Michelangelo«). **i** Via Corrado del Greco 11, tel. 0584/757325.

Stazzema   The natural mountain village crowns a hill beneath the tower-like Monte Procinto in the south of the Apuane Alps. The Romanesque church Santa Maria Assunta stands at the entrance to the village.

Tereglio   The fortified town stands watch over a deeply-cut Apennine trench merging with the central Serchio valley south of Barga. Access to Orrido di Botri.

Torre del Lago   The greatest attraction in the small town on Lago di Massaciuccoli (5km south of Viareggio) is the museum-like villa of opera composer Giacomo Puccini (1858 – 1924), who is also buried here. Opera stage on the lake, opportunity to take a boat ride.

Vagli di Sopra, Vagli di Sotto

Two old stone-cutting villages in the northern Apuane Alps (access via Poggio in Garfagnana): The lower of the two is situated on the reservoir of the same name, the upper one at the foot of the rocky Pizzo d'Uccello. By the way, the reservoir is drained every 10 years, revealing the ruins of the sunken village of Fabbriche di Careggine (the next time will be in 2004).

Vallombrosa

Established in 1013 like a fortress, the monastery grounds are hidden in the wooded western slopes of Pratomagno to the east of Florence; the monastery was mentioned in the 17th century by John Milton in *Paradise Lost*. The monastery apothecary and the forestry museum are worth a visit.

Vagli di Sotto in the Apuane Alps.

Vernio

North of Prato at the southern portal of the 18-km long railway tunnel Galleria dell'Appennino. Parco Museo del Bisenzio.

Viareggio

The most popular resort of Versilia was created in the 19th century from a fishing village around Torre Matilde. Most of the ostentatious hotels, villas and baths along the promenade, some with an Oriental flair, were erected after a fire in the year 1917. Famous carnival (since 1873). **i** Viale Carducci 10, tel. 0584/962233.

Vicchio di Mugello

Near the village, located east of Borgo San Lorenz in Mugello, Giotto di Bondone (1266 – 1337) and Fra Angelico (1387 – 1455) were born – the latter is the subject of the Museo dell'Arte Sacra e Religiosità Popolare Beato Angelico in the Palazzo Pretorio.

Vinci

The old village around a tower-like castle on the southwestern slope of Montalbano would be worth a side-trip, even if it weren't for its great son. Noteworthy sites: Museo Leonardiano, Museo Ideale Leonardo da Vinci. The birth house of Leonardo da Vinci (1452 – 1519) is situated 4km to the north. **i** Via delle Torre 11, tel. 0571/568012.

Zeri

Hiking and winter sport area amid the gentle wooded hills of western Lunigiana, on the border to Liguria.

Italian Expressions for Hikers and Mountain climbers

acqua	water	montagna	mountain (range)
a destra	right	monte	mountain
aiuto!	Help!	museo	museum
albergo	hotel	nord	north
alta, alto	high	ovest	west
ambiente	environment	paese	village
a sinistra	left	passeggiata	walk
basso	low	passo	pass
bivio	turn-off	pian	plain
bosco	woods	piazza	square
caccia	hunt	pizzo	mountain peak
caduta di sassi	falling rock	poggio	hill
cammino	path, trail	ponte	bridge
capanna	hut	pozzo	shaft, whirl-
casa	house		pool hole
cascata	waterfall	prato	meadow
castello	castle	profondo	deep
cave	quarry	rifugio	shelter hut
chiesa	church	ristorante	restaurant
cima	tip	salita	ascent
colle	hill, pass	sasso	rock, rocky
costa	mountain ridge		mountain
cresta	crest	sella	shoulder,
discesa	descent		saddle
dislivello	difference in	sentiero	path, trail
	elevation	soccorso alpino	mountain
est	east		rescue
fermata	bus stop	sopra	up
fiume	river	sorgente	source
foce	notch (mouth)	sud	south
fontana	fountain	tempo	(walking) time
fonte	spring, fountain	torre	tower
fosso	trench	torrente	mountain torrent
grotta	grotto, cave	trattoria	inn
itinerario	route, way	vetta	tip
lago	lake	val, valle	valley
lontano	far	vallone	deep valley
lungo	long	vicino	close
marmo	marble	via	road, way
metro	metre	via ferrata	fixed rope route

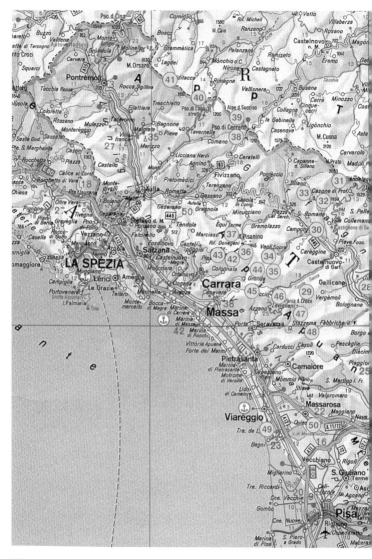

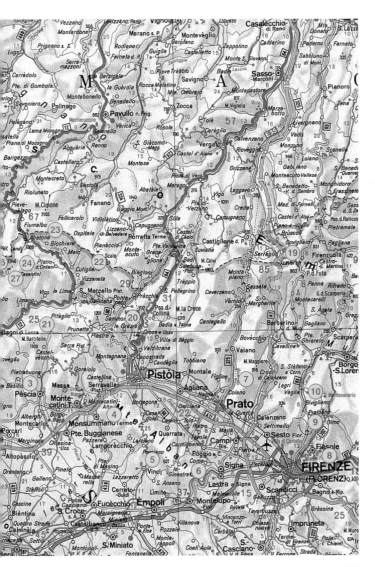

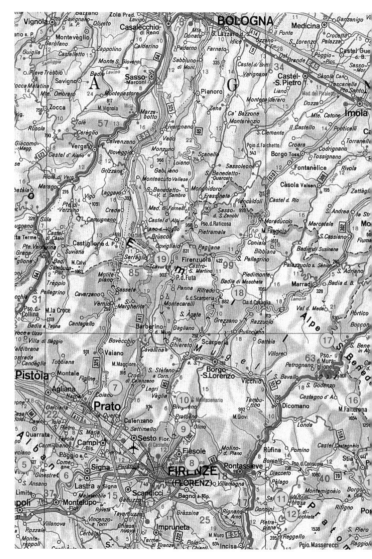

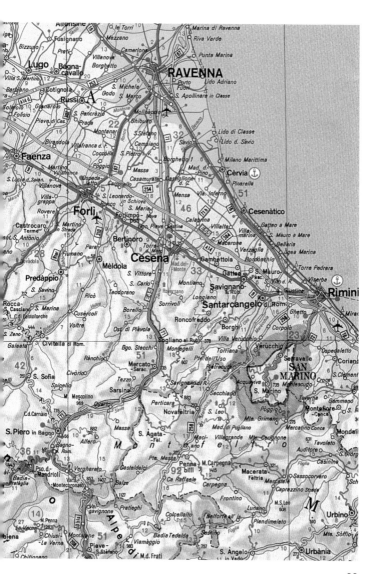

From Pisa to Florence

In terms of geological periods, it was not all that long ago that the Monti Pisani, the hills to the east of Pisa reaching up to 900m in altitude, emerged from an ocean bay. Throughout the ages, the Argo and the Serchio have deposited incredible amounts of scree and fine sediment ever farther to the west – this not only formed the plain in the confluence area of both rivers, but also the boggy basin around the flat hills of Cerbaie between Lucca and Empoli. The construction of canals led to the attainment of fertile cultivation land, which, especially in Valdinievole, the »foggy valley« south of Pescia, has developed into a centre of flower cultivation: The area surrounding the city of Lucca is not only famous for its wonderful villas, but also for the most beautiful camellia in Europe.

Beneath the partially wooded, partially karstically bare Monti Pisani, but also along the edge of »Pescian Switzerland« and the beautiful woods of Monte Albano, which rises 600m between Pistoia and the Arno, olive trees and grapevines thrive. This is the beginning of the »classical« Tuscan countryside, which stretches to the south, in Chianti, and to the east, over

Farmland and baroque gardens in one of the most beautiful cultivated landscapes in the world.

Corn poppies bloom in the valley of the Arno at the beginning of May.

the hills surrounding Florence: a lovely walking area near world-famous art treasures. On the other side of the thickly-settled basin between Pistoia and Florence, the picture is contrasted by the foothills of the Appennine: The quarries of the dark Monteferrato near Prato are the source of the green marble which decorates so many churches in Tuscany, while the nearby Monti della Calvana to the east are characterized by barren, karst hills where only grass and brush grow above the 700m line.

In the east, the area surrounding Florence is ultimately bordered by the mountain range of Pratomagno. As the name indicates, boundless meadows spread over its 1400 to 1500-m high ridge; below them, the terrain is dominated by forest. It is also the hiding place of the Vallombrosa monastery, which in the 19th century, was the first »mountain town« discovered by English tourists – a cog railway even steamed up from the banks of the Arno until 1930.

NATURE RESERVES NORTH OF THE ARNO

The Padule di Fucecchio south of Montecatini Terme and Pescia is the last of the great swamps in Valdarno Inferiore; 150 species of birds live here. However, of its 1800 hectares, only just over 10% is protected. Not far from it, Lago di Sibolla shimmers in the sunlight, accessible via wooden footbridges. It is surrounded by the most species-rich swamp in Tuscany and a »floating« high-moor bog. East of the Monti Pisani are the small remains of a riverside forest, the Bosco di Tinali, and the deciduous woods of Montefalcone and on Poggio Adorno. On Pratomagno, there is a 1279-ha deciduous and coniferous forest area around Vallombrosa under protection as a nature reserve: Here, you can find the most beautiful stand of firs in Italy, with some towering more than 55m high. The forestry garden of the monastery is one of the largest in Italy (3000 trees, 1200 species).

1 Rocca di Verruca, 537m

The solitude of the Monti Pisani

Certosa di Calci – Montemagno – Monte Verruca – Torre degli Upezzinghi – Certosa di Calci

Starting point: Certosa di Calci (also called Certosa di Pisa), 39m, near Calci.
Access: From Pisa or Lucca to San Giuliano Terme, there, take right to Calci and to the Carthusian monastery: 17km and 31km respectively.
Walking times: Certosa di Calci – Montemagno 1 hr., up Monte Verruca 1½ hrs., descent 2 hrs.; total walking time 4½ hrs.

Ascent: 500m.
Grade: Easy walk on (barely waymarked) streets and forest trails; only the narrow, rocky paths around the summit require sure-footedness.
Refreshment: Trattoria in Montemagno.
Map: Carta Turistica e dei Sentieri »Monte Pisani – Colline Livornesi«, Multigraphic Firenze.

Only a few kilometres separate the commotion around the Leaning Tower and solitude: »O beata solitudo, o sola beatitudo« is written over the gate to the baroque Carthusian monastery of Calci. It is just as quiet beyond, on the Monti Pisani: The massive castle on its southernmost foothill, the rocky head of Monte Verruca, has long fallen to ruin – only a single, weathered stone statue on the edge of the path is reminiscent of its former splendour. However, the magnificent view over the mountains, to the Arno and to the sea has endured.

Adjacent to the **Carthusian monastery**, the Via degli Omberaldi leads between olive gardens towards the village of **Montemagno**. At a turn-off to the

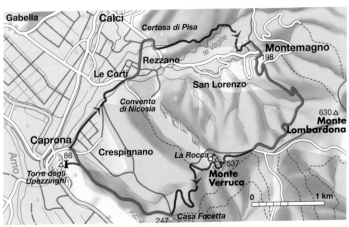

right (arrow on ground), head down, then to the right, to a small car park: To the left of a garage, an old path begins, which leads into the forest trench of the Rio Spareti and past a **mill** to further young plantations. At the next fork, turn left, then right into Via di Cerbaiola. Head right on an asphalt path over a trench, then to the left, and in front of a gate passageway, to the left up Via Poggio di Montemagno. Head right on a path leading uphill between gardens, then left on Via Paganelli through two arches into the

Weathered sculpture along the way.

village centre, 198m. Before the uppermost left-hand bend to the church, the narrow Via di S. Martino branches off; it leads through a trench to the **cemetery**. Before the cemetery, head left uphill; at the following turn-off, go straight (past the roadblock) and, walking on a concrete path, upwards, snaking through olive groves. At another roadblock, head sharply to the right onto a sand and gravel road into the forest. We pass an old house, and after an extensive ascent, reach a **saddle with a fork in the road**, 420m. We walk straight on, toward the rocky summit, and soon turn left onto a narrower path, reaching a **rest area**. Continuing on an overgrown »jungle path« – the last part of it leads steeply over rocky steps to the **Rocca** gate on **Monte Verruca**, 537m. Caution: shafts! Our descent also begins at this gate; however, we go behind it to the right and around the walls on the south side. Then, we struggle through an equally steep and over a brief spot where some scrambling is required to the saddle on the other side of the summit (crossing; one could walk here comfortably along the forestry road from the saddle below Rocca). We now follow the street which initially leads over the **forest ridge** and after a short descent, turns to the left at an old **stone statue**. Stay to the left at a fork. After several turns, we reach a forest saddle and the dilapidated **Casa Focetta**, 247m, over which a power line crosses. Here, head right and down the wide forestry road (do not take the forest path turning off sharply to the right). Do not turn off anywhere until, on a small plain (water tanks, driveway), there is the opportunity for a short side-trip to **Torre degli Upezzinghi**. Then, continue downhill along the road. After a roadblock on the left, turn off sharply to the right immediately afterward, and walk through a turnstile on the embankment path in the direction of Nicosia. Pass by a factory to Via Nicolosi. Head left next to the stream onto the paved Via Buozzi to the **Carmelite convent**. There, turn left, cross the main road and head back to the **Carthusian monastery**.

2 Around Lucca

Walking on the wall

Passeggiata delle Mura and city circuit tour

Starting point: Lucca, Piazzale Ricasoli (near the train station in the south of the city).

Access: On the Autostrada Firenze – Mare (bus connections to Florence, Pisa or Viareggio). Lucca lies along the Florence – Pisa and Viareggio railway line.

Walking times: Stroll along the city wall 1 hr., city circuit tour at least 2 hrs.; Total walking time 3 hrs.

Ascent: Negligible with the exception of

climbing the 44-m high Torre Guinigi (230 steps!).

Grade: City stroll.

Refreshment: Bars and ristoranti in old city.

Map: A free city map is available in the tourist office in Piazzale Verdi (near the Porta Via Emanuele).

Tip: You can borrow audio tour guides (similar to a cell phone) for a city tour at the tourist office in Piazzale Verdi.

The 4.2-km long and 12-m high city wall of Lucca, built between 1504 and 1645, is one of the best-preserved fortifications in Europe. The only battles on its bulwarks nowadays relate to football goals, while countless citizens take a siesta under the plane-trees on the crest of the wall. You can even explore the fully accessible wall by (rental) bicycle. The view is magical – of the alleged 99 churches of this seat of the bishopric, between which the streets still run as they did in ancient times (one square even has the oval shape of a Roman amphitheatre), but also of the surrounding mountains.

We recommend starting the tour of the **Passeggiata delle Mura** from the **Baluardo San Colombano** in the south of the city (passageway from the Piazzale Ricasoli), and walking in a clockwise direction – e.g. over the Porta

The planted city wall runs behind the tower of the San Frediano church.

San Pietro, the Baluardo San Paolino, Porta San Donato, Baluardo Santa Croce (after which a peek into the park of the **Palazzo Pfanner** is worthwhile), the Piattaforma San Frediano (with a view to the church of the same name), Porta Elisa and Baluardo della Libertà (after which there is a view of the botanical gardens).

A suggestion for a stroll through the city (one of many interesting routes): Baluardo San Colombano – **Duomo San Martino** (among other items, it houses the famous Volto Santo cross) – Piazza San Giovanni – Piazza del Giglio – Piazza Napoleone – Via Vittorio Veneto – **San Michele in Foro** – Via Roma – Via

Tower view at 44m in altitude.

Fillungo (pretty shop façade)– Via Sant' Andrea (with a side-trip through Via del Carmine to **Piazza Anfiteatro**) – ascent of the **Torre Guinigi**, upon which seven stone oaks grow (beautiful panorama of the city) – Via Guinigi – Via Santa Croce – Via del Fosso (adjacent to the stream running through the city)– Baluardo San Colombano.

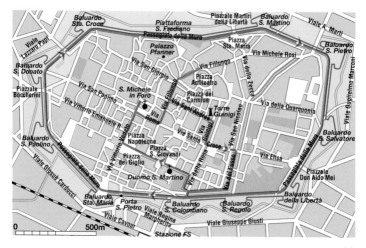

3 From Collodi to Pescia

From the baroque garden to the city of flowers

Collodi – Colle Terminetto – Monte a Pescia – Pescia

Starting point: Collodi, 125m, car park in front of the garden of the Villa Garzoni.
Access: On the Autostrada Firenze – Mare to the Chiesina Uzzano exit. From there, to Pescia and left to Collodi: 12 km. Pescia's railway station lies on the Florence – Lucca railway line. Return from Pescia to Collodi by bus (leaves from the Piazza XX Settembre in the south of the city).
Walking times: Collodi – Monte a Pescia 2 – 2½ hrs., descent to Pescia 1 hr.; total walking time 3 – 3½ hrs.

Ascent: 450m.
Grade: Easy mountain walk on roads, forestry and paved pathways.
Refreshment: Bars/ristoranti in Collodi, Monte a Pescia and Pescia.
Alternative: From Pescia back to Collodi on foot: from the former monastery San Michele in the southwestern part of town to marker no. 460 over the Rio Dilezza valley, 1 hr.
Map: Carta dei Sentieri e Rifugi No. 21/22, Multigraphic Firenze.

This tour is hard to do with children – the Parco di Pinocchio is too attractive to the little ones. The originator of the wooden liar is from the village built up high on the slope (and he called himself by the same name). Grown-ups, however, will surely enjoy the forest and panorama walk to the lovely town of Pescia in Valdinievole (Valley of Fog).

Pinocchio's home: the village of Collodi.

To the left of the **garden of the Villa Garzoni**, we ascend the paved Via di Castello to **Collodi**. We head steeply up to the **church** and the **Castello**, where we reach the asphalt road on the right (intersection): Heading left past a car park, we travel on the gravel road in wide turns through grapevine and olive gardens up into a wooded valley. Head straight on at a **cross** (arrow: »Percorso«) onto the **Colle Terminetto**, 501m. There, we turn right, go over the stream and, around two turns, arrive at a fork (Crocalino Alto), 540 m: Head straight ahead downhill on the forestry path, turn left at the next fork, and, following the turns (near the power line), down into a wooded valley. Cross

Once a year, the old town of Pescia is beautifully lit.

the meadow floor, pass a house, and finally on a paved road to **Monte a Pescia**, 319m. Turn left and go to the car park below the church (Ristorante; to the right, a side-trip up to the church). Following the arrow and the red and white markers on the asphalt road down to a **red house**, pass it on the right, and head downhill in steep curves on a partially overgrown cobble-stone path (mind the coloured markers on the olive trees). After passing a **cross**, turn right, pass old villas and arrive at the **gate of the city wall**. Pass the Villa Cafaggio and enter the old town of **Pescia**, 62m. Take a bus back to Collodi.

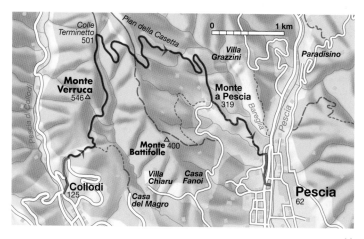

4 Monsummano Alto

The village above the giant quarry

Thermal Bath Grotta Giusti – Monsummano Alto – Cava Grande – Thermal Bath Grotta Giusti

Starting point: Monsummano Terme, thermal bath Grotta Giusti, 60m.
Access: On the Autostrada Firenze – Mare to the Montecatini exit. From there via Pieve a Nievole to Monsummano Terme and on the Via di Grotta Giusti (sign) to the thermal bath: 3 km.
Walking times: Grotta Giusti – Monsummano Alto 1 – 1½ hrs., descent 1 – 1½ hrs.; total walking time 2 – 3 hrs.

Ascent: 300m.
Grade: Easy walk on roads and wide paths.
Refreshment: Bars and ristoranti in Monsummano Terme and Monsummano Alto, spa hotel at the thermal bath.
Map: Carta Turistico – Escursionistica Montalbano e Padule di Fucecchio, S.E.L.C.A. Firenze. Folder (sketch of the route) at Monsummano tourism office.

Porta del Mercato enables access to Monsummano Alto.

15km southwest of Pistoia, between the Appennine and Montalbano, the thermal springs of Montecatini and Monsummano bubble. The highly fashionable spa facilities lie at the foot of two villages that crown their hills like eagle's nests. That of Monsummano Alto was used as a quarry for centuries – the »Cava Grande« stretches almost up to the summit, fortified like a castle.

From the rear section of the car park next to the **Grotta Giusti** thermal bath, a gravel road leads up to a transformer tower (sign: »**Percorso geologico**«, marker 30). In front of a house, turn right and head to a fork at the edge of the wood: Turn right and continue on the geological instructive trail, passing two old quarries, and go left between terraces, up to a dilapidated farm. Soon thereafter, we reach the **La Vergine chapel**, where we head left into the wood on an asphalt road (sign: »Chiesa di San Nicolao«). Ignore the following turn-off. At the second turn-off, go left onto the wooded and meadow path to Porta del Mercato, and further upward to the Romanesque church of **Monsummano Alto**, 340m.

Walk through the village to the tower (car park) and downhill for a short distance on the asphalt road. Then, go left on a meadow path to

Casetta Pellegrini, and along a concrete and gravel path to an asphalt road, 153m, onto which we turn left downhill. Caution: Take the second gravel road that turns off to the left and heads up into the wood. The road leads gently up and down, passing several **quarries**, and at some old buildings, turn left to the giant **Cava Grande**. Head right in a bend and left above the street on a path leading into the woods. After a short descent, go left downhill along a cobblestone path. We pass another quarry and, beneath **Cava Rossa**, arrive at the familiar fork at the foot of the mountain. You can also »do« the **Percorso Vita** which turns off to the left – it leads through a cypress wood and around a small valley to the thermal bath.

A view of the countryside: From the watchtower, you can see as far as the Appennine.

5 Around Vinci

On the trail of the universal genius

Vinci – Anchiano – Santa Lucia – Faltognano – Fonte del Sassone – Santa Lucia – Vinci

Starting point: Vinci, 97m, Municipio in Piazza Leonardo da Vinci.
Access: On the expressway from Florence– Pisa/Livorno to Empoli. There, cross the Arno and follow signs to Vinci: 13 km. Empoli lies on the railway line from Florence – Pisa; from there, there are bus connections.
Walking times: Vinci – Anchiano – Santa Lucia 1 hr., circuit walk via Faltognano 2 hrs., Return route to Vinci 1 hr.; total walking time 4 hrs.

Ascent: 500m.
Grade: Easy walk on roads and wide paths, only a short part along a narrow and steep path. Always follow marker no. 14.
Refreshment: Bars and ristoranti in Vinci, in Anchiano, there is often the opportunity to buy products typical of the region.
Map: Carta Turistico – Escursionistica Montalbano e Padule di Fucecchio, S.E.L.C.A. Firenze. A free folder (sketch of the route) in the tourism office in Vinci.

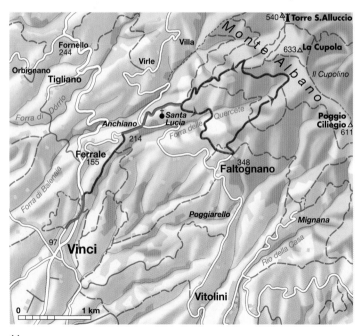

Leonardo's world view: Vinci.

How must the area around Montalbano have looked when, on 15 April 1452, a little boy saw the light of day in a modest house on a south-western slope? Most likely, not much has changed since Leonardo's childhood in these rolling hills, with their vineyards, countless olive trees and bright red corn poppies lining the paths.

We pick up the trail in front of the castle of **Vinci**, the **Castello dei Conti Guidi**, and then stroll along the narrow Via del Castello to the northern access road, which we follow 250m uphill. In a left-hand curve, continue straight ahead on the narrow **Strada Verde** (sign: »Casa Natale di Leonardo«, marker 14), through olive gardens to the main road, and turn right on it, following it to Leonardo's birth house in **Anchiano**, 214m.

At the nearby intersection, head straight on, up the steep dead-end road (sign: »Leccio di Faltognano«) to the church of **Santa Lucia**, 300m. A bit further up are the houses of the village – there, path no. 14 branches off to the right. We walk through meadow-covered slopes to a wayside shrine and into the trench.

Caution: Turn right in front of the old mill and head downhill along the slippery path to the stream (**Forra delle Quercete**), and on the other side, up over the steep wooded slope, until you reach a house between terraces. Continue on the gravel and asphalt road, then head left uphill to the Santa Maria church near the 100-year-old holm-elk of **Faltognano**, 348m. Here, go left (sign: »Fonte del Sassone«) and uphill along the wide path no. 14 to a forestry road. Go left on the forestry road, and at the next fork, straight on along the edge of the wood. Then, take another left and head up the gentle hill through the wooded slopes (spring) to the turn-off to **Torre San Allucio**, 490m. A side-trip to the former hermitage is not especially worthwhile, so we turn back to the left and descend the forestry path in the direction of »Vinci« back to **Santa Lucia**. The remaining return route follows the ascent route.

Above Faltognano.

6 From the Arno to Artimino

To the »Villa of the Hundred Chimneys«

Railway station Carmignano – Artimino – Villa Artimino – Necropoli – railway station Carmignano

Starting point: Railway station Carmignano, 36m, in the Arno valley between Signa and Empoli.

Access: By train on the line from Florence – Pisa. By car from the motorway exit Firenze-Signa on the expressway to Signa, there over the Arno and under the railroad tracks, then left and along the railroad tracks: 14 km.

Walking times: Railway station Carmignano – Artimino 1½ hrs., descent 1½ hrs.; total walking time 3 hrs.

Ascent: 250m.

Grade: Easy walk on roads and paths; hardly any of it is marked, and there is little shade.

Refreshment: Ristoranti in Artimino.

Map: Carta Turistico – Escursionistica Montalbano e Padule di Fucecchio, S.E.L.C.A. Firenze.

The eye-catcher of this walk is the Villa La Ferdinanda, built in 1594, near Artimino. The route through the ancient cultivated area via the Arno valley also leads to the remains of the 52-km long wall around Barco Reale, the hunting area of the Medici at Montalbano, and to a few Etruscan gravesites, excavated in the spring of 2000.

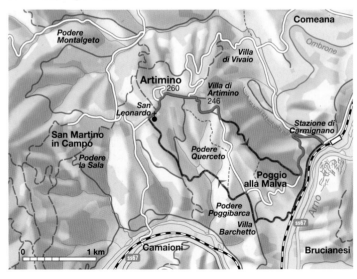

The »Villa of the Hundred Chimneys«.

From the **Carmignano railway station**, a gravel road near the railroad tracks leads to the left out of the valley (sign: »Campo Sportivo«, marker 1 A). At the attendant's hut, go left, and after the **sports field** (before the pond), head right. Follow the field path uphill and go left to a farm. Head right on the asphalt road to a house, and left to a small chapel near the Villa Barchetto. There, turn sharply to the right and walk along the gravel road past a house. At another chapel, there is an intersection: Head left on the unpaved road through a hollow to **Podere Poggibarca**, 119m. Before it, turn right, and at the next fork, left, onto the upper field path (chain) to an abandoned building, and left down to a pond. Go over the dam and right onto a steep field path, uphill between vineyards. Below a clump of trees, head right, then left onto the ridge, and continue right along the ridge. Soon, a gravel road leads to the left into the wood and past vineyards, then right onto a path to the cemetery, and left onto an asphalt road to the Romanesque **church of San Leonardo**.

Go right on the road to nearby **Artimino**, 260m.

From the gate, head along the straight avenue to the **Villa La Ferdinanda**. Pass it to the right (in the direction of »Poggio alla Malva«) and, after the bus stop, go left on the gravel road (marker 1B) into the woods. Continue straight on through a burned section of wood, then left and past an old pond. At the following fork, go straight on down to the **Necropoli di Prato Rosello**, 209m. Go around a hill on the left (water tanks), and walk along a path through the Macchia to the asphalt road on the left that leads to the **Ombrone** and the railway station.

Purely medieval: Artimino.

7 Over the Monti della Calvana, 818m

The flower mountain over Prato

Filettole – La Retaia – Poggio Cocolla – Monte Cantagrilli – Filettole

Starting point: Filettole, 142m, small village to the east and above Prato.
Access: On the Autostrada Firenze – Mare to the exit Prato Est. Toward Prato, in the suburb of Ponzano, go right over the Bisenzio river and under the railroad tracks, then left and along the railroad tracks. To the right, two narrow, unmarked streets lead up to Filettole: 5 km. Bus connections from the railway station.
Walking times: Filettole – Chiesino di Cavagliano 1 hr., to the cross la Retaia 1 hr., to Monte Cantagrilli 30 min., descent 2 hrs.; total walking time 4½ hrs.
Ascent: 800m.
Grade: Easy but long mountain walk on wide pathways and narrow trails not always well-marked. Hardly any shade; difficult orientation in fog.
Refreshment: None along the way; bars and ristoranti in Prato.
Map: Carta dei Sentieri e Rifugi no. 26/27, Multigraphic Firenze.

The barren peaks of the Monti della Calvana not only serve as an exquisite vista point over Prato, but it is also a natural-history jewel. The second-largest karst area of Tuscany is the location of several species of orchid; in spring, the white blossoms of wild narcissus gleam around the doline funnels.

Horses enjoy the »summer resort« high above Florence.

From the **church** in **Filettole**, we first walk along the Via Filettole over the bridge. Right afterwards, we go left (sign: »Chiesino, C. Bastone«, marker no. 26) onto an indistinct path, uphill near a house and a streambed, keeping left, onto a wider path that leads to the left in the trench. Head over the (usually dry) **streambed**, and then, along side it, higher, through terrain which is partially overgrown, until a wider path merges at a bench. A **stone sign** directs us to the left toward »Chiesino Retaia«, but right afterwards, we turn off to the right again (stone sign: »Chiesino Cavagliano Retaia«) and walk along a narrow path up to a small **church**, 468m. On this path, which has now become wider, we arrive at an **intersection**, between meadows

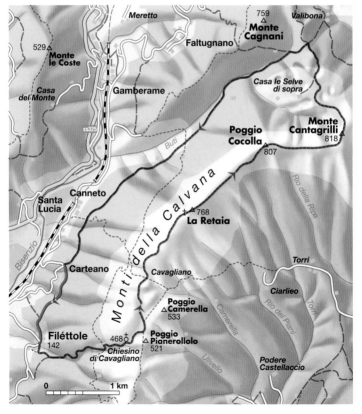

and brush: To the left, after the stone sign pointing out the direction of »Retaia, C. Bastone« and marker no. 20, head on a narrow path which is totally overgrown for a short distance, through the brush, then over meadows and a hilltop, to a **saddle with an intersecting path**, 500 m: Straight on in the direction of »Retaia, Cantagrilli«, ascend to the large **steel cross**, 752m, and continue for a short time to the summit La Retaia, 768m (beautiful view of Prato out to Florence).

Continue on the gently rolling mountain ridge to **Poggio Cocolla** (transmitter, 807m) and through a flat depression, 700m, onto **Monte Cantagrilli**, 818m.

In spring, wild narcissus light up around Monte Cantagrilli.

A striking panorama: The city of Prato spreads out 700m beneath the cross on La Retaia.

From its wooden cross, we descend over the meadow-covered ridge, keeping left (marker 20), and between doline funnels – toward **Casa le Selve di sopra** and its pond. Go past it to the right, at some distance, to a gravel road, onto which we turn right (sign: »Valibona«, towards the power line), into a saddle at the edge of the wood, 617m.

Here, turn left to the direction of »Valibona, S. Lucia, Filettole, Prato«, and head downhill on the road until you arrive just before the second gate. Caution, indistinct turn-off: Head left over a small trench (no signs, only a faded arrow), on a level path into the wood and hike downhill next to the gorge of the **Rio Buti**.

The extended, partially cobblestoned path then leads through the wooded western hills of the Monti della Calvana. Head straight on at two intersections (marker 40), and finally, between terraces, to another intersection, 152m: Left to a **stone sign**, there straight ahead on a path leading toward »Filettole«, to a house, and to **Carteano**, 161m. To the left, the asphalt road leads over a hilltop and back to **Filettole**.

8 Fiesole and Monte Ceceri, 414m

Catching your breath with Leonardo

Fiesole – Monte Ceceri – Cave di Maiano – Fiesole

Starting point: Fiesole, 295m, Piazza Mino da Fiesole.
Access: By bus (Line 7) from the main railway station in Florence. By car from the Piazza della Libertà in Florence on the Viale Don Giovanni Minzioni, through the tunnel under the railroad tracks and then to the right, following the signs to »Fiesole«: 7km.
Walking times: Fiesole – Monte Ceceri

45 min., descent to the Villa San Michele 45 min., ascent to Fiesole 30 min; total walking time 2 hrs.
Ascent: 170m.
Grade: Easy walk on wide paths and partially steep trails; lots of shade.
Refreshment: Bars and ristoranti in Fiesole.
Map: A free map is available at the tourism office.

When the heat scorches the Arno valley, it is much more pleasant 250m higher up. The Etruscans knew that, as did the Romans who left behind a large theatre on the hill of Fiesole. Not far away, a panoramic walk begins on the very mountain upon which Leonardo da Vinci may have wanted to launch experiments with flying machines. Beneath it lie the gaping historical quarries, from which a great deal of raw materials were gleaned for Florentine buildings.

Ancient quarry on Monte Ceceri.

We start at the **Piazza Mino di Fiesole** (diagonally across from the cathedral) and follow the sign »passeggiata panoramica« down the **Via Verdi**. Soon, a beautiful view of Florence opens up. Then, turn right down Via degli Scalpellini, and after 100m, right onto a gravel path alongside a wall, and into the woods. At the following three turn-offs, turn left, then right uphill, then left onto a narrow path to the memorial stone on **Monte Ceceri**, 414m. We cross the level space above the rock precipices and turn off to the right, onto the narrow path heading toward **Maiano**, which snakes steeply down between quarries (**Cave di Maiano**). Keeping left, we soon reach a wider path to the right, and head downhill between more quarries. At the next turn-off, head left, then right onto the wide path no. 7 in the direction of Maiano. Now we follow the blue and pink coloured markers along gently rolling hills through the wooded slope, until we reach a more steep descent, followed by the asphalt road to the Hotel **Villa San Michele**.

Continuing straight on, one would arrive at the nearby main road, approx. 200m (construction site); however, we go to the right, to the entry gate of the hotel. Directly in front of it to the left, we head uphill on a narrow, partially overgrown path between old walls and to a turn-off: The left path leads above the gardens to Via Doccia, which merges with Via Verdi. We follow it back to **Fiesole**.

Fiesole: Panorama over Florence.

9 Through the Parco Mediceo di Pratolino (Parco Demidoff)

Audience with the giant Apennino

Circuit walk around the park

Starting point: The main entry to the Parco Mediceo di Pratolino, approx. 300m south of the village of the same name, 470m.

Access: From Fortezza da Basso in Florence (Viale Filippo Strozzi) via the Torrente Mugnone and then right onto Via XX Settembre to Via Bolognese. Left onto it, underneath the railroad tracks, and towards »Vaglia/Bolognia«: 12 km. Bus connections from Florence (main railway station and Via Nazionale).

Walking times: Circuit walk 1 – 1½ hrs., side-trip to the »Casino« and back 1 hr.; total walking time 2 – 2½ hrs.

Ascent: Almost 200m.

Grade: Easy stroll on wide gravel paths.

Refreshment: Bar in the park.

Opening times: May to July, every Thursday through Sunday and on holidays from 10 a.m. to 8:30 p.m., in August and September to 8:00 p.m.

Map: Available at the cash desk: folder with overview map (in Italian and English).

The stone giant Apennino.

A fantastic walking experience in the woods south of Pratolino, which Francesco I. de Medici purchased in 1568, and, with ponds, waterworks and mannerist figures, had it developed into the most famous landscape park in Europe. In the 18th cent., the 30-hectare garden was renovated in new, baroque splendour, but it then declined rapidly. Only after 1814 was it renovated again, this time in the English style. Fifty-eight years later, the area was transferred to Russian prince Paul Demidoff, after whom the park is still named today. The province of Florence has administered the park since 1981.

From the **main entry**, we stroll on a wide gravel path to the **Fattoria** (estate), and in front of it, to the right, to an older building which contains a **bar**. Continue straight on to the former guest house Villetta; behind it are **Peschiera della maschera** and an artificial grotto. On the 290-m long, totally straight Viale degli Zampilli, we reach a pond with croaking frogs; to the right of it, we find an old mill. If you walk around the pond in the other direction, you will come to the **gamberaie**, a series of masoned water tanks, and to a large aviary; behind a grotto, you can find the Demidoff monument. To the right, past a giant tree, one can access the **Villa Demidoff**, renovated in 1872, and, continuing further, a chapel with a domed roof. There, we turn off to the right, down to the greatest

sight: Towering over a small hamlet, the 10-m high stone giant **Appennino** squats, built in 1579/80. We walk past him to the right, and then back to Fattoria in a semi-circle – past two strange columns with sponges from Corsica and past the **Jupiter fountain**. Finally, we also recommend a side-trip to another pond and to the classicist »**Casino**« by Montilia, a curious combination of a hunting lodge and vista point.

A palette of colour on the hills above Florence.

10 Monte Senario, 811m

Monasteries and hermitages

Bivigliano – Monte Sennario – Badia Buon Sollazzo – Bivigliano

Starting point: Bivigliano, 585m.
Access: From Florence as in Walk 9 to Pratolino, and there, right to Bivigliano: 18km.
Walking times: To Monte Senario 1 hr., Descent to Badia Buon Sollazzo 1 hr., return route to Bivigliano 1 – 1½ hrs.; total walking time 3 – 3½ hrs.
Ascent: 350m.
Grade: Easy mountain walk on roads and marked paths; only one spot in the

last section (north-west of Bivigliano) is very steep and requires a good sense of direction (however, you can also continue along the road).
Refreshment: None along the way; bars in Bivigliano.
Alternative: By car to the car park at the monastery, from there a circuit walk to the hermitages: 45 min.
Map: Carta dei Sentieri e Rifugi 26/27, Multigraphic Firenze.

At the monastery established in 1233 on Monte Sennario, you can not only taste their homemade pine liqueur, but also look out over the whole mountainous countryside in the north of Florence. In the grottos and hermitages around the summit, monks lived as hermits (overview map on the monastery terrace). And, next to a path to an even older abbey with the promising name of »Beautiful Delight«, there is a sign that even indicates the distances to Rome (305 km) or Vienna (835 km).

From Albergo La Bruna in **Bivigliano**, we walk up **Via della Fittaccia** and then continue to follow the signs pointing toward »Montesennario« (at the second left-hand curve, a short-cut route leads to the right through the forest). At the La Fornace house, go

Before the Badia Buon Sollazzo.

left to a **car park** (wooden cross): to the right, a short side-trip to a ghiacciaia (ice cellar), to the left, the asphalt road continues. In between, head through a gate and onto the gravel »Via del Silenzio e della Preghiera« to the **cemetery** and **monastery** on **Monte Sennario**, 815m.

Descend along the asphalt road. At the left-hand curve, head straight on (gate) on a forest path (marker 00, »Via degli Dei«) over the mountain ridge to a **saddle** (wooden cross). Diagonally to the left (yellow marker no. 00) to **Porticciola**,

A silent shrine: the monastery Monte Senario.

675m. To the right (sign: »Badia Buon Sollazzo«) downhill over meadows to the **Casa Sódera**. Right to a gate; behind it, go left and along the edge of the forest. Then, turn off to the right and, a short distance later, to the left through a defile down to the asphalt road. On it, go left, passing above the (inaccessible) **Badia Buon Sollazzo**, 541m, and south around the Poggio Fondello, until we veer to Bivigliano on the road. At the town sign, a path, which is very steep at the beginning, leads to the left through the wooded slope to an intersection. Go right, down to two rivulets, and at the following fork, go straight (no marker). After a clearing, go right to the first houses of **Bivigliano**, and left on the asphalt road up into the village.

11 Vallombrosa

Circuito delle Capelle, the chapel walk

Vallombrosa – Paradisino – Capella della Fonte di San Giovanni Gualberto

Starting point: Vallombrosa monastery, 958m, car park at the fish pond.
Access: From Florence via Pontassieve and Pélago to Vallombrosa: 40km (bus connections).
Walking times: Side-trip to Devil's Rock 15 min.; circuit walk around the monastery 1½ hrs., side-trip to the spring chapel 1¼ hrs., total walking time 3 hrs.
Ascent: 200m.

Grade: Easy forest walk on roads and paths that are cobblestoned but partly steep and sometimes slippery.
Refreshment: Ristorante/Pensione both in Vallombrosa and in Saltino, 1.5km away.
Map: Pratomagno – Carta dei Sentieri, S.E.L.C.A. Firenze. A free folder on the chapel route (including a sketch of the route) is available in the monastery.

In the year 1013, the noble Florentine Giovanni Gualberto Visdomini retreated into the isolated slopes of Pratomagno. He thus became the founder of a monastery which still houses monks today. Not only do they care for the famous woods (one of the beech trees is supposedly 1000 years old), but also the ten chapels around the shrine.

An invitation to pray.

From the **Vallombrosa monastery**, we first stroll along the road in the direction of Consuma over two streams and, after 300m, turn left to the **Capella del Masso del Diavolo** (stone cross, panorama). Back to the car park, we head toward the mountain, following the sign »Circuito delle Capelle / Monte Secchieta« between monastery and stream. We bear left at the fork and cross the **bridge** (waterfall) to the **Capella di San Torello**, and up the paved »Steps of Suffering« (Scala Santa), up to the **Capella del Masso di San Gualberto**. At the nearby **Capella delle Colonne**, turn right to the former **Paradisino** hermitage, 1032m (panorama from the terrace). Turn right on the road to the **Capella del Faggio Santo**, located somewhat above, and downhill to the intersection behind the monastery: Head left on a cobblestone path up toward Bocca del Lupo, but, at the next fork, bear right and walk down to the **Capella di Santa Caterina**. Go right on the road to **Capella di San Girolamo** and back to the monastery.

Finally, we walk from the main entry along the straight road, lined with trees. At the left-hand curve, we descend along the cobblestone path to the right, to another road; beneath it is the **Capella della Fonte di San Giovanni Gualberto** with its spring building. Continue to the lowest point of the tour, 842m, then turn left, crossing the street again, and up to **Tabernacolo di San Sebastiano**. Take the nearby road back to the monastery.

This spring bubbles in honour of the monastery founder Giovanni Gualberto.

12 Monte Secchieta, 1450m

View of the sunny south

Vallombrosa – Monte Secchieta – Poggio alle Ghirlande – Vallombrosa

Starting point: As in Tour 11.
Access: As in Tour 11.
Walking times: Vallombrosa – Monte Secchieta 1½ hrs., descent via Bocca del Lupo back to the monastery 1½ hrs.; total walking time 3 hrs.
Ascent: 500m.
Grade: Easy mountain walk on cobble-stone paths, forestry roads and partly steep forest trails.
Refreshment: Ristorante/Pensione in Vallombrosa, bar/ristorante at Monte Secchieta (closed Mondays), ristoranti in Saltino.
Map: Pratomagno – Carta dei Sentieri, S.E.L.C.A. Firenze.

This time, the summit is not the destination – its transmitter masts, roads and buildings are too ugly. Still, the steep ascent onto the main ridge of Pratomagno is worthwhile: for the pretty views of Casentino, and even more for the surprising panorama which opens up during the ascent over Valdarno to the hills of Chianti – and last, but not least, for the wonderful tree stands which are justifiably under protection.

From the Vallombrosa monastery, we walk to **Paradisino**, 1032m, as described in Walk 10. Behind it, on the other side of the street, we continue very steeply, following the sign »Secchieta« up through the wood. Head left to a **spring water chamber** and, subsequently, somewhat downhill. Turn left shortly before the stream (arrow) onto a narrow path. At a former charcoal-burning site with three conspicuous rocks, turn sharply to the left (arrow), and continue to the upper right on a wider forest path between heaps of boulders on the ridge of **Monte Secchieta**, 1450m (the summit itself is blocked off). Take the gravel road to the right to Ristorante Giuntini, pass a hilltop with a memorial stone for Italian resistance fighters to a turn-off near some weekend houses: Take a right (sign: »Saltino / Vallombrosa«) downhill on the forestry road, cut a bend to the right short, and at the following turn-off (La Macinaia house), continue to the right. Shortly thereafter, head left on forest path no. 13 in the direction of »Saltino«

Mountain torrent near Vallombrosa.

One of the largest and most beautiful forest areas of Italy: the Pratomagno.

onto **Poggio alle Ghirlande**, 1225m. Take a path through meadows to the small plain on Poggio Novale, 1201m. Go right into the wood and walk along the steep forestry path to the intersection at the forest saddle of **Bocca del Lupo**, 1119 m: head to the right (sign: »Vallombrosa«) downhill on a forest path, cross a forestry road and go to the next fork. Head straight ahead on an old cobblestone path down to the monastery.

Casentino and Mugello

Forest, as far as the eye can see: The basin of Casentino spreads out east of the Pratomagno, surrounded by virtually immeasurable tree stands. However, not only hermits settled the area around the old towns of Bibbiena and Poppi to renounce the world in green seclusion: When wood needed to be brought to Florence, there was a great deal of hustle and bustle around the sacred spring mountain of the Arno, the good 1600-m high Monte Falterona.

On artfully-placed slides and mule paths, the felled logs were brought to the river which carried them – bound together in rafts – with the spring floods down the valley to Florence. The best fir trees were underway for about two weeks until they reached the shipyards of Pisa, to then travel the world as ship masts.

The green world on both sides of the Sieve valley. In the background, the Appennine can be made out.

Typical Tuscany: a »procession« of cypresses.

Similarly green and fresh is Mugello, the neighbouring western catchment area of the Sieve river. This hilly area in the north of Florence was not only the birthplace of a few of the most significant artists of Tuscany, but also of the Medici family, whose reign (from the 14th to the 18th cent.) has continued to influence the appearance of the region today. They stretched their realm of influence far out beyond the main crest of the Appennine to the north – up to the austerely beautiful »Fiorentina Romagna« or »Romagna Toscana«, veined with gorge-like valleys and hardly known by tourists. In the area of the main crest, there are still remains of trenches and fortifications from the World War II: In 1944, German troops retreated behind the 320-km long »Goth line« between the Adria and Liguria. Battles with the Allies moving in from the south and the defensive action of Italian partisans cost over 200,000 people their lives.

PARCO NAZIONALE DELLE FORESTE CASENTINESI, MONTE FALTERONA E CAMPIGNA

The large national park, measuring 36 400 ha, established in 1990 in the border area between Tuscany and Emilia-Romagna, protects the natural woods on the Apennine main crest between eastern Mugello and north-east Casentino. Its heart is the primeval forest area around Sasso Fratino north of Camaldoli. The wolves that live here are all but impossible to spot; you are more likely to glimpse roe and red deer, and perhaps even the rare spectacled salamander, or one of the 80 species of birds indigenous to the area. Visitor centres are situated in Londa, San Benedetto in Alpe, Stia, Serravalle, Badia Prataglia, Chiusi della Verna, Premilcuore, Santa Sofia and Bagno di Romagna; Information centres can be found in Bibbiena, Castagna d'Andrea and Tredozio.

13 Castello di Romena – Borgo alla Collina

Romanesque architecture in a romantic countryside

Pratovecchio – Castello di Romena – Pieve di Romena – Borgo alla Collina

Starting point: Railway station Pratovecchio/Stia, 430m, approx. 1km north of Pratovecchio.
Access: From Florence through the Arno valley to Pontassieve, over the Consuma Pass up to just before Poppi, then left to Pratovecchio: 57 km.
Walking times: Railway station – Pratovecchio 15 min., to Castello di Romena 45 min., to Borgo alla Collina

1 hr., to the Porrena railway station 30 min.; total walking time 2½ hrs. Return by train.
Ascent: 350m.
Grade: Easy walk on roads, wide paths and trails; little shade.
Refreshment: In Pratovecchio and Borgo alla Collina.
Map: Pratomagno – Carta dei Sentieri, S.E.L.C.A. Firenze.

Right in the middle of Casentino, between fields and meadows, stand the ruins of the Castello di Romena, dating from the 11th cent., where even Dante was a guest. One of the most interesting Romanesque churches in Tuscany hides a short distance from here.

Coming from the **railway station** at **Pratovecchio**, we go almost 1km into the **centre of town**, and then right (sign »Castello«) to the bridge over the **Arno**. On the other side, walk along the road branching off to the right, and up to the first left-hand curve. Go right on a gravel path (marker 26) over a driveway, past the **Casa Palaia**, and back onto the asphalt road. After a good 500m, turn sharply to the left (gate), walking uphill on a trail between trees, and head right to **Casa Rontani**. Go left on the asphalt road and straight ahead on the gravel path (cypress avenue) to the **Castello di Romena**, 610m. Pass the castle wall on the left, and head right on the gravel

Only three towers have endured: Castello di Romena.

road downhill and past the **Fonte Branda**. Then, turn left onto a narrow asphalt road to the village of **Romena**; go right at the cemetery to **Pieve di San Pietro**, 476m. Continue on that road for about 1km more. Then, turn left

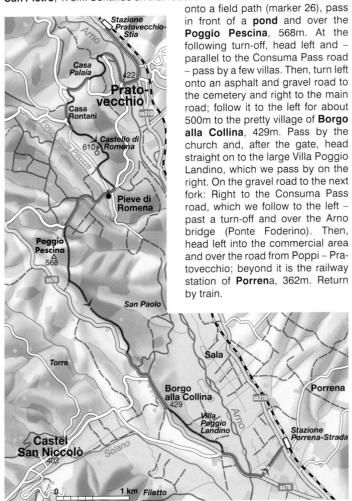

onto a field path (marker 26), pass in front of a **pond** and over the **Poggio Pescina**, 568m. At the following turn-off, head left and – parallel to the Consuma Pass road – pass by a few villas. Then, turn left onto an asphalt and gravel road to the cemetery and right to the main road; follow it to the left for about 500m to the pretty village of **Borgo alla Collina**, 429m. Pass by the church and, after the gate, head straight on to the large Villa Poggio Landino, which we pass by on the right. On the gravel road to the next fork: Right to the Consuma Pass road, which we follow to the left – past a turn-off and over the Arno bridge (Ponte Foderino). Then, head left into the commercial area and over the road from Poppi – Pratovecchio; beyond it is the railway station of **Porren**a, 362m. Return by train.

14 La Verna and the Monte Penna, 1283m

The sacred mountain of Tuscany

Chiusi della Verna –La Verna monastery – Monte Penna

Starting point: Chiusi della Verna, 953m.
Access: From Bibbiena: 23km (from Pieve San Stefano: 17 km).
Walking times: Chiusi della Verna – La Verna monastery 45 min., to Monte Penna 45 min., descent 1 hr.; total walking time 2½ hrs.
Grade: Mountain hike on wide paths and steep, rocky forest trails.

Ascent: 330m.
Refreshment: Bars and ristoranti in Chiusi della Verna, Refettorio del Pellegrino in the La Verna monastery.
Map: Carta Escursionistica Parco Nazionale delle Foreste Casentinesi, Monte Falterona e Campigna, S.E.L.C.A. Firenze.

A mountain of miracles: The La Penna boulder was supposedly split by an earthquake during the Crusades. In 1214, Francis of Assissi received it, who had been living here as a hermit, converting even bandits. In the year 1224, he allegedly received stigmata in his rocky cell. The current Franciscan monastery La Verna, which is »stuck« onto the southern side of the rock precipice, became known as the largest pilgrimage site in Tuscany – and as a magnificent vista point.

The Chiesa Maggiore (La Verna).

Next to the **Ristorante Da Giovanna** on the main road, the cobblestone »**Strada pedonale**« (sign »La Verna, La Penna«) heads upward, beneath rock walls and between old terraces. After the entrance to the National Park visitor centre, it is signposted as »**Sentiero Natura**«. Go right on the merging path heading up to a chapel. Further up, we reach a gate to the forecourt of the monastery **La Verna**, 1128m.

After viewing the monastery, we leave the covered Corridoio delle Stimmate, with its frescoes of the life of St. Francis, through the door to the left of the church portal. Behind it, a set of **stairs** leads up to **two chapels** (sign »Penna«; also accessible from the car park in front of the monastery). From there, we reach the trail marked no. 51 through a depression and more steeply along rock precipices (with a view to the »**Masso di Frate Lupo**« peak) to the chapel on Monte Penna, 1283m (exposed vista point with a railing).

On the other side, in a **notch**, cross over a **secondary summit**, 1266m, and then through the wooded slope down to a **chapel**. Cross the monastery access road and continue downhill on trail 51 (»Sentiero Natura«) through a valley (Fondo della Melosa) lined with mossy rocks. In front of a precipice, go left to a gate, and then turn off to the right, then to the left onto a cobblestone path to a building, from where you can walk down to the ascent path and thus the nearby starting point.

Fertile land and barren erosion fields alternate beneath Monte Penna

15 From Camaldoli onto the Monte Penna, 1331m

In the tranquillity of Foreste Casentinesi

Camaldoli – Eremo di Camaldoli – Passo dei Fangacci – Monte Penna

Starting point: Camaldoli monastery, 813m.
Access: From Bibbiena towards Badia Prataglia / Cesena, after 9km – before Serravalle – go left to Camaldoli: a total of 14 km.
Walking times: Camaldoli – Eremo di Camaldoli 1 hr., to Monte Penna 1½ hrs., descent 2 hrs.; total walking time 4½ hrs.
Ascent: 600m.
Grade: Easy mountain walk on roads,

steep paths, mostly shaded.
Refreshment: None along the way; pilgrim hospice and sale of monastery products in Camaldoli.
Map: Carta Escursionistica Parco Nazionale delle Foreste Casentinesi, Monte Falterona e Campigna, S.E.L.C.A. Firenze.
Alternatives: Start at Sacro Eremo or Passo dei Fangacci (total walking times 3½ or only 1 hr. respectively).

Nestled amid the expansive beech and chestnut woods of the upper Casentino is the Camaldoli abbey, established in 1046, which is still run by the Camaldoli Order. The walk to the 300-m high hermitage of the monastery, and further to Monte Penna, which offers a surprising panorama to the north of the banked-up Lago di Ridracoli, provides an idea of the contemplative solitude into which the monks once retreated.

From the **Camaldoli monastery**, 813m, we walk upwards on the asphalt road through the **Fosso Camaldoli** and past a chapel. Further up, a steep path (marker 68) provides a short-cut to the turns. Above a rest area, walk a short distance on the road to **Sacro Eremo di Camaldoli**, 1103m. From there, we follow the asphalt road rising to the right, and a short-cut forestry path on the left (sign »Prato alla Penna«). After about 500m, trail no. 74

The reservoir of Ridracoli beneath the mountains of the northern side of the Appennine.

branches off to the left: It leads up through the wooded slope to the saddle at **Prato alla Penna**, 1248m. Go right over the road and follow marker 00 further uphill. At the turn-off to Poggio Tre Confini (the side-trip to the completely wooded summit is not worth it), bear left and down to the **Passo dei Fangacci**, 1228m.

From the (closed) hut on the road, head right around a hill into the nearby saddle **Aia di Guerrino**, 1219m. There, bear left (sign »Monte Penna«) and initially follow path no. 00 uphill, then left,

The Camaldoli hermitage.

following marker 225 under layered sandstone rocks into a saddle, 1274m. Lastly, turn right onto the steep ascent path to the top of **Monte Penna**, 1331m.

The return follows the same route, whereby you can also walk from the Passo dei Fangacci on the level dirt road to Prato alla Penna.

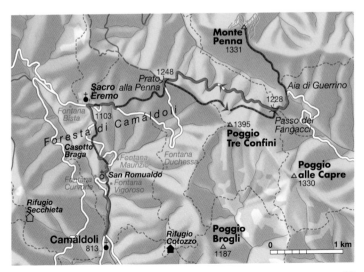

16 Monte Falterona, 1654m

Over the sources of the Arno

Fonte del Borbotto – Monte Falco – Monte Falterona – Fonte del Borbotto

Starting point: Fonte del Borbotto, 1210m, rest area with shelter above Castagno d'Andrea.
Access: From Florence via Pontassieve to Dicomano, toward Forlí up to San Godenzo and to the right to Castagno d'Andrea: 46km. The curvy access road to Fonte del Borbotto is paved for 4 more km, followed by 2km of gravel surface. Bus connections to Castagno d'Andrea; from there, you can access the starting point on foot in 1¼ hrs.
Walking times: Fonte del Borbotto – Passo Piancelli 45 min., to Monte Falterona 1 hr.,

descent 45 min.; total walking time 2½ hrs.
Ascent: 450m.
Grade: Easy mountain walk on roads and paths; mostly shaded.
Refreshment: Osteria in Castagno d'Andrea.
Alternative: You can also start directly at the Passo Piancelli; access from Stia in Casentino via Passo La Calla: 20 km.
Map: Carta Escursionistica Parco Nazionale delle Foreste Casentinesi, Monte Falterona e Campigna, S.E.L.C.A. Firenze.

Many springs have their sources on Monte Falterona – one is the source of the Arno.

Monte Falterona, in whose southern flank is the source of the Arno, was considered a sacred site as far back as ancient times. Its popularity has endured, because, especially on weekends, entire processions surge up to its summit cross. From there, you have a view of the entire Casentino and

Horizontal sandstone layers characterize the mountain countryside north of Monte Falterona.

the neighbouring Pratomagno, up to the environs of Florence, while the front, northern summit meadow offers a wonderful panorama of the endless forests of the Appennine and the layered rocks of the Balze delle Rondinaie. From the **Fonte del Borbotto rest area**, we walk along the gravel road or on short-cut paths to La Stufa and then, in two bends, through the wooded slopes of Monte Falterona to **Passo Piancelli**, 1500m (car park). Head right onto a forest path (»Pista del Lupo«) in the direction of »Monte Falco, Montefalterone« in a depression and past the spring **Sodo de Conti**, to a meadow saddle on the main crest. Go right (sign), following marker 00 to the almost totally wooded **Monte Falco**, 1657m. Continue downward over the ridge and bear left onto a defile along the slope to a turn-off:

Bear right onto a steep and narrow trail up to the rocky crest, and to the northern meadow of **Monte Falterona**, 1654m. Between beech and mountain pine trees, we reach the wooden cross in the southern summit meadow in a few minutes.

Return to the first meadow; there, bear left onto trail no. 16, heading over a forest ridge and in several serpentine curves down to the gravel road.

Go left on the road to reach the nearby starting point.

17 Monte del Prato Andreaccio, 991m

Woods, meadows and waterfalls

San Benedetto in Alpe – Prato Andreaccio – Monte di Londa – Balze Trafossi – Cascata dell' Acqua Cheta – San Benedetto in Alpe

Starting point: San Benedetto in Alpe, 495m, car park next to the bridge in the centre of town.

Access: From Florence through the Arno valley to Pontassieve and via Rufina and the Passo del Muraglione to San Benedetto in Alpe: 60km (from Forlì: 45km).

Refreshment: None along the way; bars and pizzeria in San Benedetto.

Walking times: San Benedetto – Prato Andreaccio 1½ hrs., over Balze Trafossi to the waterfalls of Acqua Cheta 1 hr., to San Benedetto 1 – 1½ hrs.; total walking time 3½ – 4 hrs.

Grade: Challenging mountain hike; narrow and partly very steep paths (slippery when wet).

Ascent: 600m.

Refreshment: Bars and pizzeria in San Benedetto.

Alternative: Hike only to the waterfall, start at the sign »Cascata Acqua cheta mulattiera« (2½ – 3 hrs. there and back).

Map: Carta dei Sentieri e Rifugi 25/28, Multigraphic Firenze.

On the thickly-wooded Alpe di San Benedetto over the Passo del Muraglione, the Tuscan border reaches over the main crest of the Appennine in the direction of Romagna. On the northern side, the National Park encompasses a very remarkable waterfall that – at 70m in height – tumbles over the layered rock wall in several strands (and once inspired Dante Alighieri).

Shady, but steep!

Two ways there begin in San Benedetto, at the bridge over the mountain torrent **Acqua Cheta**. We start at its upper end (in the direction of the pass), where a set of **stairs** leads down to a **chapel**. From there, we follow trail no. 409 towards the valley and upwards through steep wooded slopes. After **Pianellona**, 680m, we must traverse two exposed gullies. Suddenly, the markers point sharply to the left: The trail now snakes extremely steeply uphill, and then turns right just as abruptly. Finally, having crossed a ridge growing beech trees and reached a wider path, we arrive at the summit meadow of **Monte del Prato Andreaccia**, 991m.

Continue onto a saddle, 978m, and through the wooded slope to the ruins of **Casa Monte di Londa**. We mostly keep near the wooded crest of Monte di Londa to **Balze Trafossi**, 929m. Head left, down to a small meadow, passing house ruins, and descend steeply to a brook, which we jump over. From the meadow in the mountain valley of **I Romiti**, 720m (ruins of a hermitage founded in the 11th cent. by monks from Vallombrosa), follow marker 407 down to the water-

On the Alpe di San Benedetto.

fall of the tributary brook **Cà del Vento**. Balance on stepping stones and cross the flow-off water to a fork, 678m (view to **Cascata dell' Acqua Cheta**). Turn off to the right and head downhill to an old mill and a rest area. After a more steep ascent, the partly cobblestone path leads over **Fosso dell' Acqua Cheta** and past a stone hut; at a fork, keep down to the right. At a rest area, go right, down to the brook and, walking along it, out to **San Benedetto**.

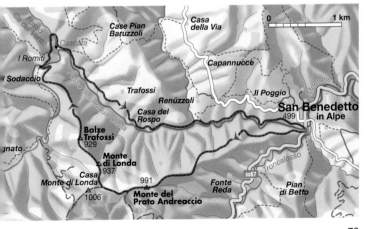

18 Val d' Inferno – Torrente Rovigo

Fairy-tale gorge and waterfall pool

Badia di Moscheta – Vall d'Inferno – Cascata del Rovigo

Starting point: Badia di Moscheta, 569m, above Firenzuola.

Access: As in Tour 9 from Florence to Pratolino and further to San Piero a Sieve, then towards Firenzuola via Scarperia and the Giogo di Scarperia to Rifredo; there, to the right on the narrow road to Badia di Moscheta: 47km (from Imola via Firenzuola: 59 km).

Walking times: From Moscheta to the bridge below Casetta di Tiaro 1 hr., to Cascata del Rovigo 1 hr., Return route to

Moscheta 2 hrs., total walking time 4 hrs.

Ascent: 400m.

Grade: Shady forest walk; wide paths and small trails.

Refreshment: Ristorante at Badia di Moscheta.

Alternative: If you only wish to walk to Cascata del Rovigo, start at the bridge beneath Casetta di Tiaro; Access from Firenzuola: 8 km.

Map: Carta dei Sentieri e Rifugi 25/28, Multigraphic Firenze.

Due to higher amounts of precipitation, deep gorges formed in Pietra Serena on the northern side of the Appennine, from which horizontally-layered sandstone is still collected today in large quarries. One of these

In the Val d'Inferno.

dusty troughs branches in its upper portion into two remote canyons, which can be easily explored.

From **Badia di Moscheta**, we follow marker 713 past the **cemetery** to the nearby **Torrente Veccione**. Turn right in front of the stone bridge to an old **mill**, head uphill on a trail and through rocky narrows into the wooded **Val d'Inferno**. Head over a side trench to the bend of the valley, along the stream and then up to the dilapidated **Case Val d'Inferno**. Behind it, the path forks: Head left under old chestnut trees down to the mouth of the **Torrente Rovigo**, 464m. From the bridge (on the other side, a steep path to the village of **Casetta di Tiara**), head straight ahead on the gravel road in the direction of »Cascata del Rovigo«. Bear right up a steep concrete path, turn right again across

Destination waterfall: the Torrente Rovigo.

from the **mill**, then left (sign »Cascata«) over the **footbridge**. Turn right, continuing along the stream and past the last houses. In a left-hand curve, head straight on up trail 711 and through the wooded valley. After about 1.5 km, turn right in the direction »Cascata«, through the streambed and, ultimately, to the right across the water to the **Cascata del Rovigno**, 600 m: The small waterfall spills into a magical pool under curved, layered sandstone. Return via the same route.

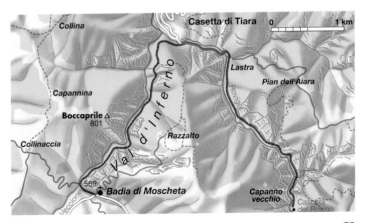

19 Sasso di Castro, 1276m

The block of rock over Firenzuola

Il Faggiotto – Cima del Sasso di Castro

Starting point: The red ANAS house in Faggiotto, 920m (at stone km marker 50 on the road leading high above the valley over Passo della Futa).

Access: From Florence over the Passo della Futa: 50km (from Bologna over the Passo della Raticosa: 51 km).

Walking times: To Sasso di Castro 1½ hrs., descent 1 hr.; total walking time 2½ hrs.

Ascent: 380m.

Grade: Mountain hike on narrow and partly rocky trails which, however, pose no special difficulty.

Refreshment: None along the way; ristorante at the Passo della Futa.

Alternative: From the Passo della Futa to the cross on Monte Gazzaro, 1125m (2½ hrs. there and back).

Map: Carta dei Sentieri e Rifugi 25/28, Multigraphic Firenze.

From the Passo della Futa, which, during World War II, attained sad notoriety as a bulwark of the bitterly contested »Goth Line«, the Appennine emanate a strange, dark rocky mountain crest to the north. It is serpentine

The ascent to Sasso di Castro, in the background Monte Rosso.

On old trails high above the Firenzuola basin.

rock that formed millions of years ago in undersea eruptions. It also forms parts of Sasso di Castro. The angular block provides a wonderful view of the austere, thinly settled valley basin of Firenzuola.

At the **ANAS house** in Faggiotto, a gravel road with the marker 737 begins that leads up through the woods to a small **plain**. There, a trail turns off to the left which leads level on the open slope. On the partly-walled route between small rock formations (beautiful view downward) we arrive at a **ridge** covered in fir trees, 1023m. Here, turn sharply to the right and walk along curves over the partly rocky, partly wooded slope to the wooden cross on **Cima del Sasso di Castro**, 1276m.

The descent follows the same route.

Through the Mountain Country of Pistoia to the central Serchio Valley

Winding valleys, old villages and gently rolling wood and flower-covered mountains – such is the Appennine in the »hinterland« of Pistoia. In the northeast of the province, the summit altitudes approach 1000m, to the west, they rise over 1900m high. There, jagged rocks (such as the 700-m high eastern precipices of Corno alle Scale) can be seen, as can the traces of Ice-Age glaciers that left large cirques and small glacier mills (whirlpool holes). From the large hills above the Lima valley, one can see as far as Montblanc on clear days, and to the Julian Alps, and across the sea to Corsica.

Between the mountains, many historical trails snake from the Po plain into Tuscany – from Via Giardini Ximedes via Abetone to Porrettana, the first railway route to Tuscany. In 1625, the dukes of Tuscany from Lucca and Modena agreed to the construction of the Via dei Remi, the »Road of Oars«: The shipyards of Pisa required large amounts of beech wood up into the 18th cent., which was felled around Cutigliano and brought to Garfagnana beneath the Alpe Tre Potenze, named for the »three powers«. Up to just a few years ago, similar cobblestone paths had been the only connection to a

View from Monte Rondinaio over the Alpe Tre Potenze to Monte Cimone (to the left on the horizon).

Lago Santo beneath the northern flank of Monte Giovo is actually situated in the bordering province of Modena.

few secluded mountain villages in northern Pistoia.

Memories of economic specialities such as steel processing (ore from the island of Elba is used for this) or the production of natural ice (the snow collected in winter was solidified in walled-up ice cellars and stored till summer) are still alive in several small museums.

NATURE PRESERVES IN THE MOUNTAINS OF PISTOIA

The three bordering natural reserves of Abetone, Campolino and Pian degli Ontani are situated northwest of Cutigliano, and have a total area of 1272 ha. In this region, old, untouched deciduous and coniferous woods can be found, among them the only natural fir stand of the Appennine (only accessible via a guided tour). The 243-ha large Riserva Naturale Acquerino, known for its wealth of rare plants, is located northeast of Pistoia; it stretches from the valley of Limentra Orientale to the 1239-m high Poggio di Chiusoli.

20 Porrettana Trekking

Pistoias »Railway Trail«

Pracchia – Passo di Piastreta – San Mommè – Castagno – Piteccio

Starting point: The Pracchia railway station, 607m.
Access: The best route is from Pistoia by train; return from San Mommè or Piteccio.
Walking times: Pracchia – San Mommè 2 – 2½ hrs., further to Piteccio 1½ – 2 hrs., total walking time 3½ – 4½ hrs.
Ascent: 350m ascent, 650m descent.

Grade: Easy mountain walk on partly insufficiently or non-marked roads, paths and trails; lots of shade.
Refreshment: Bars in Pracchia, Prato al Lago, San Mommè, Castagno and Piteccio.
Map: Carta dei Sentieri e Rifugi 21/22, Multigraphic Firenze.

In 1864, the first railway line was opened from the Po plain to Tuscany: The »Porrettana« – named after the resort of Porretta Terme – connects Bologna with Pistoia. A 2.5-km tunnel was drilled through the main crest of the Appennine; however, the 500m difference in elevation on the steeply plunging southern face could only be surmounted with the aid of wide bends, high bridges and a number of other tunnels. Thus, this stretch of track is reminiscent of the most beautiful alpine railway lines. A ride along this pretty countryside should be coupled with a walk back through the varied low mountain ranges, on which you will find virtually undiscovered details: Railway stations frozen in a time, wells to supply steam engines with water, or

A rest on the »rock clearing« of the Passo di Piastreta.

A bunker in the forest? No, a tunnel ventilation shaft (Pozzo No. 2).

the »Pozze«, those walled ventilation shafts through which the smoke escaped from the tunnels: Pozzo No. 3 – accessible as a short side-trip and covered with an iron grate – is an astounding 223m deep!

From the **Pracchia railway station**, walk next to the road heading out of the valley toward the centre of town. After about 250m, turn right and pass under the railway tracks. Pass by a **water filling station** and a sports field, then take the gravel road uphill (old marker signs), passing a **well**. At the following turn-off, bear left, continuing on the asphalt road, to the cone-shaped **Pozzo No. 2** (here, we recommend a side-trip to **Pozzo No. 3** along the forestry road branching off to the right). Right after it, in a left-hand curve, head straight on, then right over the stream and uphill on a narrow, partly walled trail straight across the steep slope (a part of it has slid down). At the point where you can look down into the valley to Pozzo No. 3, a wider path merges: Take it upwards through the woods, over several trenches to the rocky **Passo di Piastreta**, 897m. Continue to the left, and at the following turn-off, go straight ahead and then uphill to the left. In front of a fence, turn right onto the forestry path to a **pond**, and after a roadblock, bear right (sign »Parcheggio«) to a **meadow** (Lagoni). There, head left, then right again immediately afterwards, downhill in the direction of »Pistoia«, and to the right, along the fence to an asphalt road. Turn right onto this road (sign

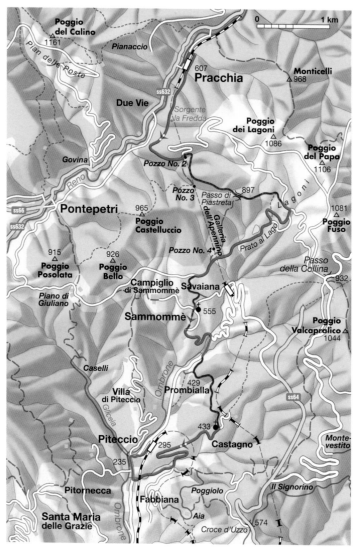

82

»Lago«), downhill in curves to **Prato al Lago**. Bear right to the small lake (bar), pass it to the left on a path and head to a gravel road that leads steeply downhill through the forest (stream ford). At some houses (well), an asphalt road begins (on the right, the dilapidated Pozzo No. 4). Finally, a path provides a short-cut to the curves, and we reach the church of **Sammommè** (also San Mommè), 555m.

On the left, the road leads to the **railway station** 800m away. We walk along Via Crocetta to **Pro Loco** and bear right downhill along the overgrown cobblestone path. Further down, an asphalt path leads into the valley. Pass above the **Torrente Ombrone** then turn off to the right (you can also get here from the Sammomè railway station). Shortly thereafter, turn left (sign »Vezzosi«) onto a gravel road leading uphill, then turn left again to **Prombialla**, 429m. Beyond the houses, turn left onto a narrow, red and green-markered trail leading between terraces, into the forest and – passing a chapel – to **Castagno**, 433m. Pass the **church**, then head down to the town on a cobblestone path. Further down, cross the stream to the asphalt road that leads down into the valley to the right. At the turn-off to Fabbiana, bear right and continue along the stream. Passing under the high railway bridge, we reach **Piteccio**, 235m. Turn right on the road heading into the valley, then right up to the **railway station**.

The impressive viaduct of Piteccio in an engraving from 1864.

21 Penna di Lucchio, 1176m

Even a fake Switzerland has a real mountain

Pontito – Croce a Veglia – Penna di Lucchio – Monte Memoriante – Pontito

Starting point: Pontito, 745m, in »Pescian Switzerland«.

Access: From Pescia on the curvy road via San Quirico and Stiappa: 17km (bus connections).

Walking times: Pontito – Penna di Lucchio 2½ hrs., crossing to Monte Memoriante 1 hr., descent 2½ hrs.; total walking time 6 hrs.

Ascent: 500m.

Grade: Challenging mountain tour with easy but airy climbing passages (I) requiring sure-footedness and a head for heights. Trail marked in the summit area.

Refreshment: None along the way.

Alternative: You should only climb the neighbouring Monte Memoriante, 1151m, if you were able to climb Penna di Lucchio without shaking. Two climbing routes (II) lead through the wall structure to the summit plateau – the direct route (arrow »diretta«) over exposed rock steps and through the steep gullies near a remarkable tower, or to the left (faded colour markers) over exposed rock belts, passing underneath a cave and through a grassy shallow basin: 1 hr. there and back.

Map: Carta dei Sentieri e Rifugi 21/22, Multigraphic Firenze.

In the northern part of the hilly hinterland of Pescia, a jagged set of peaks surprises the visitor, some of which have been formed from steeply folded rock layers, which, geologically speaking, belong to the higher mountain ranges on the other side of the Lima river. To get us going, we climb on steep stair-like paths through the medieval village of **Pontito**. In front of the

Penna di Lucchio, southern ridge.

church (archway), go left, passing above the cemetery, and in an ascending curve, to the road which, initially still paved, leads to the left to the **Madonna delle Grazie** chapel and to the **saddle** near the **Croce a Veglia** chapel, 900m. Taking the left-hand forestry road (sign »Uso di sotto«), we walk around a hill, head straight on at the fork, and beneath Monte Granaio, follow curves into the area of **Casa Giannini**. In front of it, turn right (sign »percorso«). At the petrol station, turn right, ignoring the path branching off to the left. Then, turn right (marker 88). Descend into the **saddle** directly in front of Penna di

Pontito, the highest village in the »Svizzera Pesciatina«.

Lucchio (le Calcinaie), 946m. Hike straight on along a trail heading up over the rocky, tree-covered steep slope, then bear right to the southern ridge which is airy but has well-formed steps, adjacent to which we climb onto the secondary summit. Finally, we climb over the partly sharp connecting crest to the **main summit**, 1176m.

We descend along the initially wide, then narrow and stony north-western crest into the **forest saddle** before Monte Memoriante, 1049m. Head downhill to the left, and at the next two forks, also bear left. Pass by rocks on a level surface, then head uphill to the left on the merging path between chestnut trees and on a steep forestry path to the **saddle** before Penna di Lucchio. Return to the starting point via the ascent route.

22 To the Lago Scaffaiolo

The would-be volcano

Doganaccia – Lago Scaffaiolo – Monte Spigolono – Passo della Croce Arcana – Doganaccia

Starting point: Doganaccia, 1547m, holiday community above Cutigliano.
Access: From Lucca via Bagni di Lucca to Cutigliano: 54km. From there on the mountain road via Melo: 14km (or by cableway to the middle station).
Walking times: Doganaccia – Lago Scaffaiolo 1¼ hrs., over Monte Spigolono to the Passo della Croce Arcana 1¼ hrs., Descent to Doganaccia 30 min.; total walking time 3 hrs.
Ascent: 350m.
Grade: Easy mountain walk on roads and paths, difficult orientation when foggy.

Refreshment: Available at the middle and top cableway stations; Rifugio Duca degli Abruzzi (open all day from 25 June to 25 September, otherwise at certain times on the weekend, tel. 0534/53390).
Alternative: From Lago Scaffaiolo on hiking route 00 on to Passo dei Tre Termini, 1785m, and to Passo Strofinatoio, 1847m; from there, left onto Corno alle Scale, 1945m (wind rose, lift station, large summit cross on Punta Sofia, 1939m, situated in front): 2½ hrs. there and back.
Map: Carta dei Sentieri e Rifugi No. 17/19, Multigraphic Firenze.

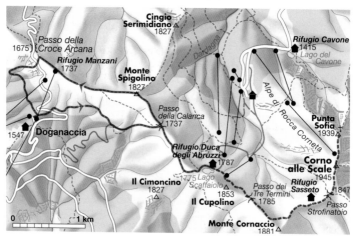

Several legends are woven around the 220-m long and 2.30-m deep Lago Scaffaiolo – especially fantastic are those linking it with the sea, and even with a volcano crater. It is, however, true that the crossings in this section of the Appennine have been known for ages: Hannibal might have crossed

Lago Scaffaiolo with its yellow »tin hut«. In the background, Corno alle Scale.

here with his elephants, the road over the Passo della Croce Arcana had already been paved in cobblestone as early as 1633, and a toll was collected in Doganaccia. Today, money is more likely to flow in winter, when the cableway and lifts are humming.

In **Doganaccia**, below the **middle station**, we walk underneath the cableway and to the small **wooden church**. Follow the marked path under a lift bridge, up the **ski trail** and, following the signs to »Lago«, up a steep, rocky path to a gravel road. Go right over the stream and follow the markered hiking path (arrow »Lago Scaffaiolo«) through the meadow slopes. Above a spring (concrete tunnel) we ascend to the **Passo della Calanca**, 1737m. Head right into the next depression and to the left of the ridge (a small lake is below), walk into a notch with a stone hut. **Lago Scaffaiolo**, 1775m, glitters in the background, under the yellow »tin can« of the **Rifugio Duca degli Abruzzi**, 1787m.

Return along the same route up to **Passo della Calanca**. Then, continue over the crest (marker 00/411) and onto **Monte Spigolono**, 1827m. Descend to **Rifugio Manzani** at the cableway top station, 1737m, and on to the **Passo della Croce Arcana**, 1675m. Bear left on the gravel road or on the markered hiking path through the ski area and past »Mary's beech« down to **Doganaccia**.

23 Libro Aperto, 1937m

A mountain like an open book

Abetone – La Verginetta – Monte Rotondo – Monte Belvedere – Abetone

Starting point: The two stone pyramids on the height of the pass of the winter sport resort Abetone, 1388m.

Access: From Lucca via Bagni di Lucca: 65km (from Modena: 94 km).

Walking times: Abetone – Libro Aperto 2 hrs., descent 2 hrs.; total time 4 hrs.

Ascent: 600m.

Grade: Easy mountain walk on well-developed forest paths and mountain trails; only the uppermost summit ascent is exposed and thus requires sure-footedness and a head for heights (however, circumvention is possible). Difficult orientation when foggy!

Refreshment: Bars/ristoranti in Abetone, Casetta di Lapo (open in summer).

Alternative: The jagged summit structure can be circumvented to the right over the meadow saddle between both peaks.

Map: Carta dei Sentieri e Rifugi No. 17/19, Multigraphic Firenze.

Alpine roses on Monte Rotondo.

The Libro Aperto over the Passo dell' Abetone really does look like an open book – the »pages« between its two panoramic peaks are formed by a wide meadow saddle. The wind rose on the highest point, Monte Rotondo, is only surpassed by the 2165-m high Monte Cimone in the north. However, the alpine roses like it here better: The Libro Aperto is its southernmost location in Europe.

From the **height of the pass in Abetone**, we walk up Via dell' Uccelliera. From the transformer station, go right, following marker 00 into the Boscolungo pine forest. From a barrier on a flat gravel road – passing under power lines – we head into a **forest saddle with wells**. Head to the right, somewhat downhill, and around Monte Maiori up onto another saddle, then in the direction of »Passo Croce Arcana« to the meadow saddle **Serrabassa** (also called La Verginetta), 1492m (rest area, Rifugio Casetta di Lapo). Bear left onto a gravel road (marker 495) to a **spring water chamber** under the silted-up Lago della Risaia. Cross a stream and walk along the forest path into the open Vallone dei Faggi, bordered by rock walls, which ascends toward Libro Aperto. Above the source of Rio Borgognoni, there is a fork: Bear left across the steep slope into a notch, 1881m. Here, turn sharply to the right and traverse

The only exposed passage on Libro Aperto is secured with a wire rope.

a few rock steps, arriving at the northernmost dome of Libro Aperto, 1932m. Walk on the grassy crest to the rock structure of **Monte Rotondo**, 1937m, which we climb over steep, downward layered rock (rope). Descend into the wide meadow saddle between the two main peaks and ascend **Monte Belvedere**, 1896m. The descent is initially without a path, then leads along a marked trail along old border stones over the hilly western crest, until we arrive beneath a wayside shrine with a madonna and once again reach the saddle La Verginetta. For the return to Abetone, by the way, the wooded Monte Maiori can be traversed or circumvented on its northern side.

24 Circuit Tour to the Lago Nero

Between ski lifts to solitude

Valle del Sestaione – Lago Nero – Foce di Campolino – Valle del Sestaione

Starting point: Rear Valle del Sestaione, 1309m, west of Cutigliano.

Access: From Lucca via Bagni di Lucca to almost in front of Ponte al Sestaione beneath Cutigliano, then left in the direction of Pian di Novello and past the (very remarkable) Orto Botanico Forestale to the end of the road at two lift stations: 62km (from Modena via Abetone and Le Regine: 100km).

Walking times: To Lago Nero 1½ hrs., return route 1½ – 2 hrs.; total walking time 3 – 3½ hrs.

Ascent: 500m.

Grade: Easy mountain hike on partly narrow, steep and not always well marked walking paths and alpine pasture trails.

Refreshment: None along the way, bars and ristoranti in Pian di Novello Cutigliano.

Alternative: From Lago Nero via Passo della Vecchina, 1823m, to the Alpe Tre Potenze, 1940m (1½ hrs. there and back).

Map: Carta dei Sentieri e Rifugi No. 17/19, Multigraphic Firenze.

A region rich in history: On the 1940-m high Alpe Tre Potenze at Abetone, the duchies of Lucca, Florence and Modena once bordered one another, and Hannibal is said to have been in the area. It was in more recent times that the invasion of skiers prevailed. It has only remained quiet on the reedy Lago Nero, on the alpine pastures of Campolino, on which one can find small Ice-Age glacier mills (marmitte), and in the neighbouring nature preserve, in which ancient Norway spruce, measuring up to 50m high, grow.

From the **lift station** in **Valle del Sestaione**, we walk along the gravel road (marker 104) further into the valley; we ignore the merging ski trail. After about 1 km, in a curve, turn off to the left onto a narrower path. Soon we must cross a small brook, then continue on a wide forest path. Take the turn-off to the right, pass the remains of a wall, and head to an intersecting path (no. 102), on which we bear left to **spring water chambers** and through a Norway spruce wood. Caution: Take a right soon after and head up through a steep trench. Go right to another water chamber, somewhat downhill, then uphill to the left (sign »Lago Nero«) on more level meadow terrain. We see a fork: Bear right up to a stone hut a short distance away; beyond it is **Lago Nero**, 1730m.

The trail turning off to the left (sign »Campolino«, marker 100/PT), on the other hand, leads across a slope with manually-planted mountain pines in the notch **Il posto dei Mori**, 1760 m: Great view down on the Orrido di Botri! Continue up and downhill through rocky slopes and over alpine pasture floors past old lift huts to **Foce di Campolino**, 1785m. Here, go left onto a narrow trail weakly marked in blue and red down to the cirque and then to the right along the former lift route to the lower huts. Continue along the ski trail (on the left, there is a hidden forest lake), then left on a wide path into the wood, and finally back onto the overgrown ski trail to the Torrente Sestaione and back to the nearby starting point.

Nebulous: Lago Nero under dark clouds.

25 Monte Giovo, 1991m

The wild side of a big mountain

Lago Santo – Valle del Fontanone – Monte Giovo – Lago Santo

Starting point: The car park before Lago Santo, 1470m, in the Parco dell'Alto Appennino Modenese near Pievepelago.
Access: From Lucca via Bagni di Lucca and Abetone to Pievepelago, from there, a short distance in the direction of Passo di Radici and left on a narrow mountain road over Le Tagliole: 88km (from Modena: 92km).
Walking times: To Monte Giovo 2 hrs., descent 1½ hrs.; total walking time 3½ hrs.
Ascent: 550m.
Grade: Challenging mountain hike requiring sure-footedness and a head for heights. Dangerous in fog or snow!
Refreshment: Ristorante Cacciatore; Rifugio Vittoria (12 beds, open from the beginning of May to mid-October, tel. 0536/71509); Rifugio Giovo (46 beds, open year-round, tel. 0536/71556); Rifugio G. Mariotti (40 beds, open year-round, tel. 0521/835909); Rifugio Tullio Marchetti (open every day from March to October, otherwise on weekends, tel. 0536/71253).
Map: Carta dei Sentieri e Rifugi No. 15/18, Multigraphic Firenze.

The almost 2000-m high Monte Giovo reflected in Lago Baccio.

From the valley of the Serchio, as seen approximately from Barga, Monte Giovo looks like a broadly curved grass crest, studded with trees far up its flanks, and striped with diagonal layers of stone. The picture is a different one from the north, from Emilia-Romagna: There, it shows off its dark northeast face, towering over the magical, almost 6-ha large Lago Santo Modenese, which owes its existence – as do all water holes in the Appennine – to the scraping effect of Ice-Age glaciers.

We reach its outlet before the car park at the Ristorante Cacciatore on a wide forest path. From **Rifugio Vittoria**, 1501m, bear right along the shore of the lake and past more huts. Then, trail no. 529/21 ascends through the beech wood. Pass a spring water chamber and head over a meadow floor to **Passo della**

Above: From Colle Bruciata, the view stretches to Monte Cimone.
The following pages: Evening ambience in Valle del Fontanone.

Boccaia, 1587m. Here, do not head left in the direction of Monte Giovo, but rather follow the GEA markers through the woods and meadows of the wide **Valle del Fontanone** to the source of the stream of the same name, and

then walk across a steep slope to **Colle Bruciata**, 1730m (before Cima dell'Olmo). There, we head left (marker 00) and over the steep ridge, which drops off on its rocky northern side, to the summit cross of **Monte Giovo**, 1991m.

The descent follows to the left on trail no. 527 through the scree cirque on the north side and over a forest ridge to **Passo della Boccaia**. Alternatively, over the airy southeastern ridge (marker 00, view down over the northeast face), for about 500m, then left on trail no. 525, which leads down through steep, rocky terrain and a wooded basin directly to **Lago Santo**.

26 Monte Rondinaio, 1964m

The spirited circuit over Lago Baccio

Lago Santo – Lago Baccio – Monte Rondinaio – Monte Giovo – Lago Santo

Starting point: As in Walk 25.
Access: As in Walk 25.
Walking times: To Monte Rondinaio 2 hrs., crossing Monte Rondinaio to Monte Giovo 1 hr., descent 1½ hrs.; total walking time 4½ hrs.
Ascent: 700m.

Grade: Challenging mountain hike with airy ridge crossing requiring sure-footedness and a head for heights (one secured passage).
Refreshment: As in Walk 25.
Map: Carta dei Sentieri e Rifugi No. 15/18, Multigraphic Firenze.

Alps or Appennine? Whatever the case, the Monte Rondinaio even satisfies seasoned alpinists – with unusual scree cirques, dark rock precipices and an elegantly curved connecting ridge to Monte Giovo. Its »key point«, although secured with a steel rope, forces one's behind out into the air, 350m above the Lago Baccio.

As in W. 25, we proceed from the **car park** at the **Rist. Cacciatore** up to Lago Santo. Caution: Just before the Rif. Vittoria, a level forest path branches sharply off to the left (to E). We follow this to a wider path uphill. From the next fork, the path to the left leads to the nearby waterfall of the Rio Baccio; however, we head straight on to **Lago Baccio**, 1554m. M. 523 directs us to the right, around the lake: Afterwards, we walk along a partly indistinct

The »Ladders to Heaven« high above Lago Baccio to Monte Giovo.

Open to the elements: Ridge hike before the panorama of Monte Rondinaio.

path to the cirque around **Fonte Acqua Fredda** and, keeping left, onto a mountain ridge (R. 521 over the lake outlet into another cirque and to the right onto the ridge). Over scree, we head to the notch **Il Passetto** and left on the stone-block ridge, or through a narrow basin to the metal cross on **M. Rondinaio**, 1964m. Back at the Passetto, we go straight on (m. 00), con-

tinuing over the ridge on narrow belts around a rocky elevation. Walk alongside the northern precipices over a grassy hilltop to the saddle **La Porticciola**, 1900m. Along steep turns, we ascend the next tower, and traverse a meadow, arriving at the wide saddle at **Altaretto**. Now we head up rock steps toward M. Giovo, along a very exposed stretch (steel rope) to a platform, and head steeply uphill to the secondary summit of **Grotta Rosa**. We take a quick walk to the turn-off of trail no. 525, and, alongside the NE precipices, reach **M. Giovo**, 1991m. Descent as in Walk 25 to **Lago Santo**.

27 Orrido di Botri

The largest trench in Tuscany

Gorge hike, only with a guide!

Starting point: Visitor centre Ponte a Gaio, 680m, at the valley end above Tereglio.

Access: From Lucca toward Bagni di Lucca to Chifenti; left via Lima into the Serchio valley and right before the railway overpass to Tereglio. Before the village, go toward Montefegatesi along a narrow road high above the valley and finally to the right, down to the visitor centre: 40 km.

Walking times: Short tour 2 hrs., long tour 4 hrs.

Ascent: Up to 500m.

Grade: Guided gorge hike on narrow sections of trail and through a streambed; only with a climbing helmet (supplied).

Refreshment: Ristorante in the Visitor Centre Ponte a Gaio (only Sun.).

Map: Carta dei Sentieri e Rifugi No. 18/20, Multigraphic Firenze.

The southern incline of Monte Rondinaio and the Alpe Tre Potenze harbour one of the greatest natural wonders of Tuscany: The Rio Pelago has dug a 4-km long, up to 500-m deep and partly very narrow gorge. Following heavy rain or during periods of melting snow, the stream still demonstrates its original strength today. The moist and cool micro-climate on its banks is home to rare plants that otherwise only grow in higher elevations. The thickly-wooded side slopes of the canyons give refuge to groundhogs and wild goats, and the rock walls even harbour l' Aquila, the eagle. Thus, the entire area was declared a *riserva naturale* in 1971. The Orrido di Botri may only be accessed from mid-June to the end of September in connection with guided tours! The guides start off daily between 9:00 a.m. and 5:00 p.m. on easy 2-hour or more difficult 4-hour tours; reservations are recommended for Sat./Sun. (tel. 05 83 / 80 00 22). Fee: about 2 and 3.50 re - spectively, per person.

The Guadina, the narrow »gate« to the rear area of Orrido di Botri.

Equipped with the obligatory climbing helmet, we climb downhill at the house near the old **Ponte a Gaio** to the stream. Directly afterwards, we have to cross the stream for the first time, either balancing

Wet feet cannot be entirely avoided – but a stick comes in handy.

along smoothly-sanded stones or wading through the cool water – there are no bridges, but several cascades and muddy pools that result in wet feet. Subsequently, we reach the narrow passage of the **Guadina**, measuring only five metres in width. A bit further back, the gorge swerves from an east/west to a north/south direction – the upper section, with its waterfalls, is called **Solco Grande** (large gully).

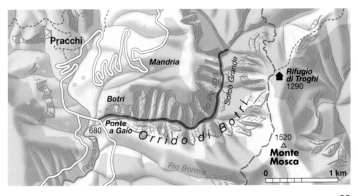

28 Barga

»Passeggiata trekking panoramica«

Circuit walk around the village

Starting point: Barga, 410m, Porta Macianella o Reale.
Access: From Lucca in the direction of Castelnuovo di Garfagnana; access road from Fornaci and Castelvecchio Pascoli: 38km from Aulla: 73 km). Barga lies on the Lucca – Aulla railway line (railway station 3.5km beneath the village).

Walking time: Including a stroll around town 1 – 1½ hrs.
Ascent: 100m.
Grade: Walk along roads, paths and a partially narrow trail.
Refreshment: Bars, ristoranti in Barga.
Map: Carta dei Sentieri e Rifugi No. 18/20, Multigraphic Firenze.

High above the Serchio valley sits the medieval village of Barga. Before having a stroll through its winding lanes, we recommend a pleasant, short walk around the village, as it conceals a few surprises.

From the information sign next to **Porta Macianella o Reale**, follow the marker »Passeggiata trekking panoramica« across **Piazzale del Fosso**, up the stairs next to the large **cedar** and the monument,

Creatively-designed park above the roofs – with a view to Pania della Croce.

The green world around Barca: View from the »Passeggiata panoramica«.

and, at the driveway of the Albergo/Ristorante Villa Libano, turn left. Take the **Via del Sasso**, branching off to the right, and go down the narrow stairs to the left. Walk along the narrow trail through a forest of reeds, downward between old olive gardens, and then left, on a level path passing under conglomerate rocks. Beneath the **arches of a supporting wall**, head uphill once again until you pass under a veranda and arrive at the Via della Fornacetta. Go left to the **Porta Macchiaia** and, before it, take a right into Via dell' Acquedotto to the old **aqueduct**. Go to the right, into Parco Kennedy, and across the playground. Pass under the new and the old **road bridges**, then take a left across the wooded slope, and left over stairs to the main road (Circonvallazione), which we reach at the Parco Bruno Buozzi. Take the road to the **old town**, and traverse it to reach the Romanesque **cathedral**.

The Duomo San Cristoforo houses a beautiful marble pulpit.

Garfagnana and Lunigiana

Far bella figura: Northwestern Tuscany is home to the most beautiful mountains! The wide valleys of the Serchio and Magra are charming in their appealing contrast between the dark Apennine main crest, made of diagonal sandstone layers, and the light limestone peaks of the Apuane Alps. In both places, the highest summits of the region display an incredible variety of forms of terrain: Monte Prado, at 2054m the culmination point of the Tuscan border crest, curves up over gentle hills full of blueberry bushes, while the Crinale dei Laghi, at over 1800m, forms a sharp knife edge between wild rock precipices over Lunigiana and the cirques of the northeastern slopes, rich in lakes. The Apuane Alps offer even more diversity – from the meadow floors around the 1317-m high Monte Matanna in the south, to the threateningly steep grassy flanks of Monte Pisanino, 1947m, in the north. Monte Sumbra, 1764m, is conspicuous due to its high, strangely rounded rock

As green as it gets: Lago di Vagli beneath the mighty Monte Sumbra.

PARCO NATURALE DELL'ORECCHIELLA

The 5 218 ha-large nature preserve around the limestone mass of Pania di Corfino in the north of Castelnuovo di Garfagnana stretches to the main crest of the Appennine (Monte Prado). On the once-cleared elevations, approximately 10 million (!) trees have been planted, and a strict hunting ban has allowed the animal world to diversify again – since 1972, even wolves have returned. Interesting tourist sites include the visitor centre above Corfino and the Orto Botanico, located directly at the foot of Pania di Corfino.

flanks, on the 1888-m high Monte Cavallo, curious stone columns jut into the air, and Pizzo d'Uccello has an impressive 700-m high north face.

Riches were hardly able to be gleaned from the winding valleys and thick chestnut woods beneath the mountains – those who could not get by in agriculture or high-elevation marble quarries had to leave. In addition, Lunigiana suffered under the constant skirmishes surrounding the strategically significant »Franconian Road«, while the mountains of Garfagnana were the setting for bitterly disputed front ground on the »Goth Line« in World War II. It has only been in recent years that primarily the area around Castelnuovo Garfagnana has developed into a popular hiking area. Especially beautiful excursion destinations include the Oricchiella Nature Reserve and the former shepherds' settlement of Campocatino, which is situated on a beautiful panoramic balcony above the Vagli reservoir.

PARCO REGIONALE DELLE ALPI APUANE

The approximately 40-km long mountain chain of the Apuane Alps was declared a Regional Park in 1985. It encompasses an area of 54 000 ha between Lucca and southern Lunigiana, Versilia and Garfagnana. Especially in the northern and central areas of this craggy limestone and marble mountain chain between Monte Sagro and Monte Corchia, nature conservation and nature utilisation go hand in hand: Isolated reserves for rare plants and animals are situated alongside marble quarries stretching almost to the mountain summits. The southern portion of the Apuane Alps is less damaged, and in parts, heavily karstic: At Monte Croce and beneath Pania della Croce, deep clefts open up, the Grotta del Vento is open to tourism, and the Antro del Corchia (1200m deep, 70km of it explored) is one of the largest cave systems in Europe. Regional Park visitor centres await you in Castelnuovo Garfagnana, Forno di Massa and Seravezzal.

29 Pania della Croce, 1858m

Limestone giant and karst wonder

Piglionico – Rifugio Rossi – Pania della Croce – Borra di Canale – Piglionico

Starting point: Piglionico, approx. 1100m above Gallicano.

Access: From Lucca to Gallicano (dir. Castelnuovo di Garfagnana): 38 km. From there in dir. of Molazzana and before the town, go left toward Alpe San Antonio, before it left in the dir. of Piglionico. After about 11 km, the asphalt road ends, gravel road approx. 2km to chapel.

Walking times: To the Rifugio Rossi, depending on starting point, 1½ – 2 hrs., to Pania della Croce 1 hr., descent depending on route selected 2 – 2½ hrs.; total walking time 4½ – 5½ hrs.

Ascent: 700 or 800m.

Grade: Challenging mountain hike requiring a head for heights and sure-footedness in scree-covered terrain.

Refreshment: Rifugio Enrico Rossi (20 beds; open daily from 20 June to 10 September, otherwise staffed on most weekends, tel. 0583/710386).

Map: Carta dei Sentieri e Rifugi No. 101/102, Multigraphic Firenze.

Two mighty mountains typify the southern Apuane Alps: the Pania Secca, wrapped in steep rocks, and the higher but more easily accessible Pania della Croce. Between them, the fossilised facial features of the »Uomo Morto« can be made out, which juts upward over a small karst plateau and has clefts of up to 300m in depths and a wild scree chasm.

Take the gravel road to **Capelle Piglionico**. From there, we walk straight on (sign: »Rifugio Rossi«, marker 7) along a forest trail – it is level at first, then heads uphill in several bends. Beneath Pania Secca, cross a grassy slope to **Rifugio Rossi**, 1609m. Continue to **Foce Puntone**, the saddle beneath the »Uomo Morto«, 1611m. Go straight (sign »Pania Croce«) and at the next fork, go right onto trail 126 across the scree-covered **Vallone dell' Inferno** up to the summit ridge. Head left across the rocky ridge edge to the summit cross of **Pania della Croce**, 1858m.

Descend along the same route up to Foce Puntone. Here, turn left (sign »Borra di Canale«) and walk along the narrow trail no. 139 beneath a rock wall into the steep

The Pania Secca.

Surrounded by rock: the cosy Refugio Enrico Rossi.

area of scree and down between Pizzo delle Saette and the craggy Vetricia mountain plateau. Traverse the laborious stretch through scree and between large boulders across the long, stepped cirque (pay attention to the coloured markers), until you ultimately walk down into the wood to the right. Head left across a wider area of scree and beneath rock walls to intersecting path 127, which we follow to the right. We follow the steadily rising and falling path, which is steeper toward the end, to the chapel and thus back to the ascent route.

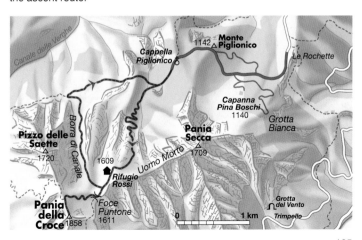

30 Across the Ponte della Villetta to Sambuca

The great bridge over the Serchio

Poggio – Sambuca – Sillicagnana – Villetta

Starting point: Poggio railway station, 400m.

Access: We recommend arriving by train from Lucca or Aulla. By car, as in Walk 28 from Lucca to Poggio: 57km (from Aulla: 48 km); to the railway station, head toward Aulla/Camporgiano for a short distance. Return from Villetta by train.

Walking times: Poggio railway station – Poggio-Sambuca 45 min., to Sillicagnana 45 min., to the Villetta railway station 1 hr.; total walking time 2½ hrs.

Ascent: 200m.

Grade: Easy valley walk on roads and paths. If you tend to get dizzy, it is better to keep your eyes on the railroad tracks while on the bridge.

Refreshment: Bars in Poggio, Sillicagnana and Villetta.

Alternative: From Sillicagnana on the road to San Romano, there, go left toward »Camporgiano« and left on an asphalt side-street down to the Serchio. Head upstream along the gravel road, across the bridge, and to the other side to the Ristorante Mulín del Rancone; from there to the Camporgiano railway station. An additional 2 hrs.

Map: Carta dei Sentieri e Rifugi No. 101/102, Multigraphic Firenze.

Bridge vista I: The Serchio, the lifeline of Garfagnana.

In the heart of Garfagnana, there are two major eye-catchers: Small, dark rocky mountains of volcanic origin, and the Ponte della Villetta. The long railway bridge also offers a footpath secured by railings across the Serchio – at a dizzying height and directly in front of the medieval village jewel of Sambuca. From the **Poggio railway station**, head along the road, then left onto a cobblestone path up to the main road. Go left across from the new church into the **village centre**, 451m. Next to a house with a loggia, go right down Via delle Vigne to vineyards. In front of a shed, go left to an oak tree, then right onto a road which leads to the large **railway bridge**. After crossing it, go right downhill along a gravel road, and on it, turn sharply to the right and under the bridge. Directly afterward, head left on a meadow trail (chain) through gardens and past a little house with a water container. In front of a farm, go right up an asphalt road. There, turn left, cross a stream, and at a wash house, turn left to **Sambuca**, 395m. Beyond the village, head right onto a gravel road toward a fence, at a sign, head right, and on the red and white marked path upward along stone walls. Walk through brush to a gravel road (sign), go right for a short way, then left. Pass a small house and – with an increasingly beautiful view of the Apuane Alps –

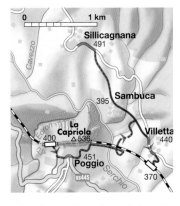

walk to **Sillicagnana**, 491m. Go back to **Sambuca**. From there, follow the asphalt road to **Villetta**, 440m, and go right to the railway station, 370m.

Bridge vista II: Sambuca, between rocks of volcanic stone.

31 Monte Prado, 2053m

To the »roof« of Tuscany

Radici Pass Road – Passo Bocca di Massa – Monte Prado

Starting point: Il Casone di Profecchia, 1314m, on the curvy road to the Passo delle Radici.

Access: From Castelnuovo di Garfagnana via Castiglione: 25km (from Modena: 106 km).

Walking times: Il Casone di Profecchia – Passo Bocca di Massa 1½ hrs., to Monte Prado 1 – 1½ hrs., descent 2 – 2½ hrs.; total walking time 4½ – 5½ hrs.

Ascent: 750m.

Grade: Easy, long mountain hike on forestry roads and narrow trails. Difficult orientation in fog!

Refreshment: Albergo/Ristorante di Profecchia. If you wish to divide the tour into two days, you can stay overnight at the Rifugio Battisti (open daily from mid-June to mid-September, otherwise on most weekends, tel. 0522/897497).

Map: Carta dei Sentieri e Rifugi No. 15/18, Multigraphic Firenze.

Monte Prado is the only two-thousand-metre peak in the Apennine main crest between Lunigiana and the upper Tiber valley (Alpe di Succiso, 2017m, the nearby Monte Cusna, 2120m, and Monte Cimone, 2165m, are just north of here). Thus, the gently rolling meadow summit is the highest point in Tuscany.

To the left of the **Albergo/Ristorante Il Casone**, steps lead up to the ski lift station (marker 54). Head alongside the steep lift track to a gravel road and turn right onto it, crossing a clearing. Then, a path branches off to the left (no. 54), which cuts short the bends in the road. Cross the wood and head upward along the precipitous edge across Fosso Faretta, then left on the road to Rifugio Cella, 1700m. Before it, cross the pasture (marker on the cattle-trough) and follow the branching remains of the trail to a saddle with a

View from the Appennine to the Panie.

large **cairn**, already visible from below. Head along the once again discernible path to **Passo Bocca di Massa**, 1816m, on the main crest. Go left (sign: »Monte Prato«, marker 00) and, in a gentle ascent, across the northern slope, completely covered in blueberry bushes, around Monte Cella into a crest depression. Continue across the slope, pass a small cross and arrive at a saddle. Cross a wide grass ridge into the next notch, head straight on toward Monte Vecchio and then bear right, circumventing it – toward Monte Prado. Traversing three small hills, we arrive at the Passo di Monte Vecchio, 1932m (a low stone hut to the left). Go straight on over a grass slope to a secondary summit, 2008m, and to the left across a wide ridge (passing the ruins of two shelters) to the small stone cross on **Monte Prado**, 2054m.

The return follows the same route.

The highest point in Tuscany.

32 Pania di Corfino, 1602m

The rock wall in Orecchiella Nature Preserve

Rifugio Isera – Pania di Corfino – Sella di Campanaia – Rifugio Isera

Starting point: The rest area in front of the Rifugio Isera, 1209m, above Corfino.

Access: From Castelnuovo di Garfagnana in the direction of Castiglione/Modena, after 2km (after a tight curve in a secondary trench) go left toward Corfino. Go right before the village into the Parco Naturale; go right in front of the Visitor Centre to the car park in front of Rifugio Isera: 19 km.

Walking times: Rifugio Isera – Pania di Corfino 1½ hrs., descent 1 – 1½ hrs.; total walking time 2½ – 3 hrs.

Ascent: 400m.

Grade: Short mountain hike on forestry roads and trails; the very steep ascent requires sure-footedness and a head for heights.

Refreshment: Rifugio Isera (20 beds; tel. 0583/660203).

Map: Carta dei Sentieri e Rifugi No. 15/18, Multigraphic Firenze.

The Parco Naturale dell' Orecchiella encompasses the expansive forest areas and flower meadows around the limestone massif of Pania di Corfino, which emerges as the foremost of the higher sandstone peaks of the Appennine over Garfagnana. By the way, the preserve area was created by the efforts of the local population and the forestry administration; only three small reserve areas are »official«.

The Apuane Alps surrounded by clouds rising over the summit meadow.

The way to Pania di Corfino is steep and rocky.

We walk along the gravel road past **Rifugio Isera** and through the wood, following bends (or on short-cut paths) up to the wonderfully-situated **Orto Botanico**, 1240m. At the rest area in front of it, a path branches off to the left with the marker 62 that leads between trees and straight across an area of scree to the foot of the **cliffs**. There, go right and over the steep, rocky grass slope into a grass depression. Head right to a **meadow saddle** (sign) and from there, right onto **Pania di Corfino**, 1603m. The cross is located somewhat below, on the edge of the cliffs.

Back to the **meadow saddle**, go right down into the wood and around a shallow basin to a fork. Go left to **Sella di Campanaia**, 1518m (wooden cross), around which a bounty of narcissus bloom in May. There, turn off to the left and walk along the partly cobblestoned path through a wooded valley to the bend in the gravel road, on which we head back to the starting point (the path branching off to the right also leads there along the stream).

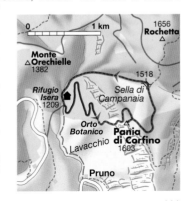

111

33 Sentiero Airone 2

A spectacle of flowers and wet feet in the Nature Reserve

Centro Visitatori – La Ripa – Fiume Rimonio – Centro Visitatori

Starting point: Centro Visitatori del Parco Naturale dell'Orecchiella, 1230m, above Corfino.
Access: As in Walk 32, but at the turn-off to Rifugio Isera, go left to the visitor centre.
Walking times: Centro Visitatori – La Ripa 1½ hrs., descent to Fiume Rimonio 1 hr., ascent to Centro Visitatori 2 hrs.; total walking time 4½ hrs.
Ascent: 550m.

Grade: Challenging mountain hike on streets and paths, partly very steep trails and in rocky gorge terrain. Be careful during high water periods – during snowmelt or after rainfall, it is often impossible to wade through the stream!
Refreshment: Bar/Ristorante La Greppia, Bar/Ristorante Orecchiella at the Visitor Centre (28 beds; tel. 05 83/61 90 10).
Map: Carta dei Sentieri e Rifugi No. 15/18, Multigraphic Firenze.

The »Sentiero Airone 2«, one of the largest yellow/blue-markered circuit routes through the Parco Naturale dell' Orecchiella, named after the outdoor magazine »Airone«, connects the elevations and the deeply-cut gorges in the west of the region. A few of the steep slopes are coloured pink in the spring – that is when countless wild peonies unfold their splendour. However, a great deal of water rushes from the Appennine at this time of year, such that the Fiume Rimonio can become a serious impediment. You should definitely plan on getting wet feet.

From the **Centro Visitatori**, we follow the blue and yellow markers of the »Sentiero Airone 2« across the street and then onto a forest path down to the springs of the **Covezza di Verrucole**. After a short ascent, we reach the **asphalt road** that leads from Piazza al Serchio into the Nature Reserve. We follow the driveway at a **wooden cross** and head to a **house**, and just after it, go right onto a meadow path into the wood. We continue straight ahead on the merging forestry road, then turn left onto a trail. At a clearing, we turn sharply to the left, cross a few brooks and head to a **meadow saddle**. Straight on along the wide path to the sparsely-wooded hilltop **La Ripa**, 1307m.

At its front edge, a narrow trail leads to the right down across the steep grassy slope. We cross a horizontally-intersecting path; further down, we turn left and then descend again straight on to the edge of the wood. There, turn left, pass above rock precipices and then, in bends, to a merging path, which we follow to the right. We first walk levelly between the rocks, then downhill to a fork: Turn right, walking across from the village of Villa to the **Fiume Rimonio**, about. 800m. We follow the mountain torrent into the valley and surmount a rocky patch. Before the **spring water chamber** beneath a rock wall, we wade through the water to the other bank. We zigzag our way up, and at the junction of a red-markered path, we turn right toward the brook again. We cross boulders and the concrete outflow pipe of the **dam** of the Lago di Vicaglia, then under a high **bridge**. Turn off to the right, head over a tributary brook and very steeply up to an old path. Turn right on it (railing) and walk down into the deep, narrow and only partly dry **gorge** of the **Fiume Rimonio**. Subsequently, we

Peonies on La Ripa.

have to cross the streambed 15 more times(!); in between, we ascend on a path and, at times, directly in scree. We ultimately cross a tributary brook up to a forestry road. Walk along it for a very short distance, turn left, then right, heading steeply across the wooded slope to a meadow. Soon after, we reach the asphalt road near the Ristorante La Greppia, 1220m. Head left to the fork, then turn right and pass the junction of a forestry road (well) to the starting point.

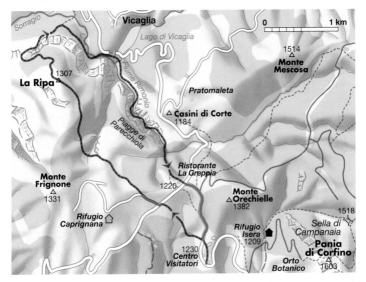

34 Hike to Campocatino

The most beautiful alpine pasture in Tuscany

Vagli di Sopra – Campocatino – Eremo san Viviana

Starting point: Vagli di Sopra, 679m.
Access: From Castelnuovo di Garfagnana to Poggio, there, go left via Vagli di Sotto to Vagli di Sopra: 17 km.
Walking times: Vagli di Sopra – Campocatino 1 hr., side-trip to hermitage and back 1¼ hrs., descent 45 min.; total walking time 3 hrs.
Ascent: 550m.
Grade: Easy walk on roads and paths.
Refreshment: Ristorante/Pizzeria Buca dei Gracchi in Campocatino (uniquely built into the rock, tel. 05 83/66 41 03).

Alternatives: Circuit walk around the Campocatino basin (trail no. 177, then Sentiero Natura): 1½ hrs. Vertigo-free mountain climbers can continue above the hermitage on trail no. 147 high above the valley; after a rest area, a surprising mini ferrata leads to a marble quarry. Descent follows gravel and asphalt road through the alpine valley of Arnetola: 2 hrs.
Map: Carta dei Sentieri e Rifugi No. 101/102, Multigraphic Firenze.

Narcissus beneath Roccandagia.

Before the impressive rocky backdrop of the 1700-m high Monte Roccandagia lies one of the most beautiful spots of the Tuscan mountain country: the Campocatino basin, dug by Ice-Age glaciers, with its archaic-looking stone huts. The shepherds who lived in them every summer have long since passed on. Today, the old houses function as weekend residences or shelters for hikers, the feathered inhabitants are cared for by the bird-protection organisation LIPU. An interesting side-trip takes us to the cave that St. Viviano (or Viano) once chose as his dwelling.

From the **Vagli di Sopra** village road, the **Via Campo Catino** (marker 7) branches off to the right: The cobblestone path leads across the wooded slope and past two chapels, up to **Campocatino**, 1000m.

After the first huts, we reach a fork: To the right, one can reach the

From Campocatino, an expansive panorama opens up to the north, stretching to the Appennine.

nearby Ristorante Buca dei Gracchi, to the left, a well. From there, we continue on the gravel road to the meadow ridge. Soon, we branch off to the left onto the »**Sentiero Natura**«. On the hill, we once again meet up with the gravel road, onto which we turn left and pass under a transmitter, then through a small birch wood to a rest area.

Then at the fork: To the left, we walk in the direction of »Eremo S. Viviano« to a pretty vista point, and head downhill in serpentine curves into a rocky trench, ultimately over steps upward underneath a large rock wall to the **hermitage** (you can borrow the key in the ristorante). Return via the ascent route.

The old shepherd's huts have become shelters for hikers.

35 Monte Tambura, 1889m

In memoriam Domenico Vandelli

Arnetola – Via Vandelli – Passo della Tambura – Monte Tambura

Starting point: Arnetola, 800m; alpine valley above Vagli di Sopra.
Access: As in Walk 34 to Vagli di Sopra. Further into the valley and through a narrow part to the access road to the marble quarry, from which a gravel road turns off: 22km (lorry traffic).
Walking times: Arnetola – Passo della Tambura 2 hrs., to Monte Tambura 1 hr., descent 2 hrs.; total walking time 5 hrs.
Ascent: 1100m.
Grade: Challenging mountain hike requi-

ring sure-footedness and a head for heights in the upper areas. Dangerous in fog or in the presence of snow!
Refreshment: None along the way, bars/ristoranti in Vagli di Sopra and Vagli di Sotto.
Alternative: If you continue straight on up the slope from the dilapidated huts beneath the Passo della Tambura, you will reach an interesting vista point (view to Sella; Tour 44).
Map: Carta dei Sentieri e Rifugi No. 101/102, Multigraphic Firenze.

The three-cornered Monte Tambura, the second-highest peak in the Apuane Alps, sits high above a historical project of prestige: Between 1738 and 1751, the Prince of Modena had a direct road built to his properties on the sea. The political situation forced his engineer, abbot Domenico Vandelli, to lay the trail across the Passo della Tambura. However, the countless,

Arnetola: An erstwhile quarry-worker's hut ducks beneath a boulder.

walled turns proved to be too narrow for the Prince's coach, which led the master builder to commit suicide.

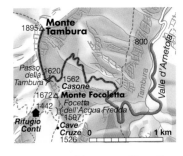

Our tour begins on the gravel road that leads into the valley end of **Arnetola** and keeps respectful distance from the giant rubble heap of the quarry. We pass a few old **stone buildings**, head uphill in bends and turn right at the two following forks. At an old concrete building, head straight on (marker 35) into the upper **marble quarry** (Cava Formignacola), approx. 1000m. At the arrow »Rifugio N. Conti«, turn left, and further up, left again and onto a gravel path up into the woods. Soon, we are walking along the **Via Vandelli**, in uphill turns, through rocky precipices and past a doline shaft to a spring at dilapidated huts (Casone), 1562m.

Go right to the nearby **Passo della Tambura**, 1620m. Continue to the right of the crest on the narrow trail no. 148. Cross rock steps into a meadow saddle (old protective trench) and zigzag across a scree-covered slope onto a rocky secondary summit. Cross the exposed ridge to the scree-covered dome of **Monte Tambura** (Vetta Tambura), 1895m. Descend along the same route.

The wind drives the clouds: A look back from Monte Tambura to the Sella massif.

36 Pizzo d'Uccello, 1781m

The wild »bird mountain«

Rifugio Donegani – Foce di Giovo – Pizzo d'Uccello

Starting point: Rifugio Donegani, 1122m, in the hindmost Valle di Gramolazzo.

Access: From Piazza al Serchio in the direction of Aulla, left in Cavalle toward Gramolazzo, along reservoir of the same name and, before the tunnel to Minucciano, go left toward Rifugio Donegani: 17km (lorry traffic).

Walking times: Rifugio Donegani – Foce di Giovo 1 hr., summit ascent 1½ hr., descent to starting point 2 hrs.; total walking time 4½ hrs.

Ascent: Almost 700m.

Grade: Challenging mountain tour; the (well-marked) summit ascent includes

exposed climbing stretches (I). A head for heights and sure-footedness are necessary. Very dangerous in fog or in the presence of snow. Hardly any shade!

Refreshment: Rifugio Guido Donegani (60 beds; open daily from May to mid-November, otherwise on weekends, tel. 0583/610085)

Alternative: Crossing Foce di Giovo – Foce Siggioli (marker 181, exposed crossing, steel rope), descent to Rifugio Donegani, 1½ hr.

Map: Carta dei Sentieri e Rifugi No. 101/102, Multigraphic Firenze.

Way up north, the Apuane Alps appear at their wildest: In addition to its highest peak, Monte Pisanino (1947m), the rocky tips of Monte Cavallo (1888m), Monte Contrario (1790m) and Monte Grondilice (1805m) tower over the springs of the Serchio di Gramolazzo, blocked by scree. The western side of the valley is dominated by Pizzo d'Uccello, which offers an energetic climbing adventure into the magical kingdom of its Dolomite needles.

From the car park next to the **Rifugio Guido Donegani**, a red-and-white marked, steep and stony path (sign »Foce di Giovo«) shortens a bend in the asphalt road. Then, turn left onto the road into the **marble quarry**. There, an arrow points to the right to a gravel road, in the direction of »Passo di

Giovo«, which winds up through the quarry in bends (pay attention to the arrows). On top, head left on a stony path into the wood and past two water tanks. Finally, a wide path zigzags into the meadow saddle of **Foce di Giovo**, 1500m (sign). We follow trail 181 branching off to the right in the direction of »Foce Siggioli«, which leads under thick beech boughs to circumvent two rocky spikes. In the next notch

The ascent route winds up across the right side of Pizzo d'Ucello.

(**Giovetto**, 1497m), go left and over the ridge, having nicely formed steps, to the peak section of **Pizzo d'Uccello**. Head through a chimney, over rock steps and, after a narrow crack, to the left onto a grassy platform (two alternatives are marked here). Bear left over an exposed ramp to a gully, which, upon exiting it, leads to the ridge. Go right on the secondary peak and over a notch to the summit cross. The descent follows the same route.

37 Via ferrata Tordini-Galligani

Climbing adventure in front of the north face of Pizzo d' Uccello

Equi Terme – Costiera di Capradosso – Ugliancaldo – Equi Terme

Starting point: Equi Terme, 250m.

Access: From Aulla in the direction of Lucca to Gragnola, there, right via Monzone to Equi Terme: 22km (from Lucca via Castelnuovo: 89 km). Equi Terme lies on the Lucca – Aulla railway line.

Walking times: Equi Terme – start of fixed rope route 2½ hrs., fixed rope route 45 min., crossing to Ugliancaldo 1¾ hrs., descent 1 hr.; total walking time 6 hrs.

Ascent: 1250m.

Grade: Challenging mountain hike with a 550-m long, exposed climbing route only secured with a fixed steel rope; absolute sure-footedness and a head for heights necessary. Very dangerous in fog or in the presence of snow!

Refreshment: Bars/Ristoranti in Equi Terme, bar in Ugliancaldo.

Alternatives: You can get around the fixed rope route by taking the gravel road to the left in front of the uppermost marble quarry (in the direction of Ugliancaldo) to a barrier and continuing a bit further in a forest trench, where the steep trail no. 192 branches off to Poggio Baldozzana. Extended circuit climbing route around Pizzo d'Uccello: From the uppermost marble quarry, go right on Via ferrata Zaccana to Colle di Nattapiana, left onto Via ferrata Piotti above Vinca to Foce di Giovo, left on the secured trail no. 181 to the Foce Siggioli and descend on the described fixed rope route – from the Rifugio Guido Donegani (Walk 36) approx. 6 hrs.

Map: Carta dei Sentieri e Rifugi No. 101/102, Multigraphic Firenze.

Marble quarries were opened up beneath the north face of Pizzo d'Uccello.

The Pizzo d'Uccello, the »Matterhorn of the Apuane Alps«, with its 700-m high north face, offers sophisticated climbing enjoyment. Those preferring solid steep ropes during vertical climbs can ascend the spirited fixed rope route established by the Pisa section of the CAI in 1971 directly across from the north face, and dedicated to the alpinists Brunello Tordini and Pierluigi Galligani. The anticipation starts in the rocky gorge from where the trident can be seen for the first time.

From the bridge beneath the historical village centre of **Equi Terme**, we hike to the right (on the southern side) along the **Torrente Lucido** on a narrow

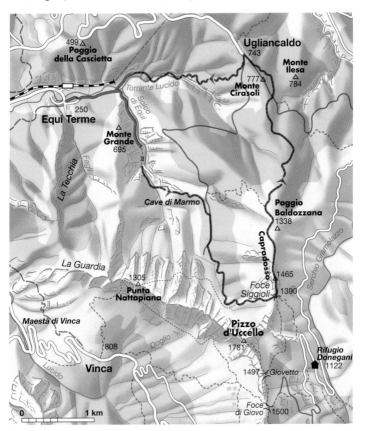

asphalt then gravel road toward the valley. Go straight at a fork, pass an old quarry and head right into the **Solco d'Equi** gorge. Go through two tunnels (between them is the chapel of the Madonna d' Equi) to a**marble quarry** (Cave Cantonaccio), approx. 400m. There, turn left, crossing the stream (sign »Ferrata«, marker 192); walk uphill between rocks and on a narrow trail through the wood to a gravel road. Turn right onto it and head toward the upper marble quarry. Just in front of it, however, turn left (chain, arrow »Ferrata«) and walk along steep curves through the grounds of the quarry to a **stone building**, 868m. Head right into the wood (arrow »Ferrata / Sent. Zacc, Sigg«), and directly afterward, turn left in the direction of »Ferrata« and walk uphill on the narrow trail beneath the north face of Pizzo d'Uccello. Walk through a washed-out gully to a **rock rib**, 980 m: From here on, the **fixed rope route** runs on the left side (downward layered rock; memorial plaque), through a sudden, steep pitch and over a sharp knife-edge of the ridge to **Costiera di Capradosso**; the route is exited near **Foce Siggioli**, 1390m. Here, go left (marker 181), across the eastern side of the rocky crest and onto the grassy **Poggio Baldozzana**, 1338m. Descend along trail 181. In the wood, continue to the right over the ridge and past a hilltop (Forticello, 998m) down to a **meadow saddle with a chapel**. From there, bear left onto the asphalt road (well) to the nearby village of **Ugliancaldo**, 743m. Behind the church, a steep descent path begins (marker TL / 176), which leads along several bends into the valley of the **Torrente Lucido** and further to **Equi Terme**.

Above: Steel ropes direct the way to Costiera di Capradosso.

Left: A dream of a village: Equi Terme.

38 Passo del Cerreto

Gentle country, wild country

Sassalbo – Passo dell'Ospedalaccio – Canale Acqua Torbida – Sassalbo

Starting point: Sassalbo, 860m, beneath the Passo di Cerreto.
Access: From Aulla on the well-developed road toward Passo di Cerreto; after 31 km, turn off at a high bridge and continue 2km to the village (from Reggio nell'Emilia: 80 km).
Walking times: Sassalbo – Passo dell'Ospedalaccio 1¾ hrs., descent to

Sassalbo 1¼ hrs.; total walking time 3 hrs.
Ascent: 450m.
Grade: Easy forest and meadow hike on varyingly wide, partially narrow and steep paths.
Refreshment: Bar and ristorante in Sassalbo.
Map: Carta dei Sentieri e Rifugi No. 14/16 or 15/18, Multigraphic Firenze.

Get ready to discover the individual character of Lunigiana: on ancient, winding pass routes between the Franconian Road and the Po plain, on alpine meadows with views stretching to the Ligurian mountains – and in scree, erupting from giant storm wounds…

Next to the church of **Sassalbo**, a road leads up to an intersection with wells. Follow the sign »Passo Cerreto« and the red-and-white marker no. 98 straight ahead to a wayside shrine, go left there uphill on a well-maintained **cobblestone path** through chestnut wood to the **Torrente Rosaro**. After

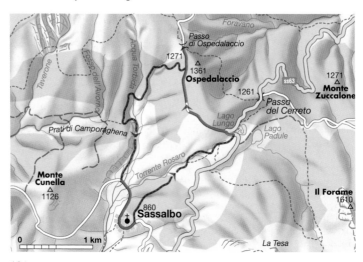

Wild beauty: the heathland at the foot of Monte Alto.

crossing the stream, the path becomes narrow and almost disappears into the meadow terrain (mind the markers). Cross a trench to reach **Cerreto road**, which we walk along to the left for a short distance to the narrow right-hand curve. There, a gravel road branches off to the left which leads across the slope of the Ospedalaccio and up to the meadow at the **Passo dell'Ospedalaccio**, 1271m.

Caution: Shortly before reaching the top of the pass, a wide **aisle** opens up in the pine forest – there is a hidden sign indicating the direction of Sassalbo here. Continue downhill on the more narrow and partly overgrown path no. 100 across the meadow lane, over small trenches and into the deeply-cut valley of the **Acqua Torbida** mountain torrent. Cross the wide gravel bed to an old access road leading to the left. After a few metres, take the forest path to the right and cross an overgrown slope. After crossing a red rock flank, we arrive at a forest ridge. Head left on the ridge down to the sparsely-grown over Prati di Camporaghena (old meadow terraces). After the hiking trail »Trekking Lunigiana« (marker TL) merges, walk straight on for a short distance onto a meadow saddle, then left across a forest trench to the Torrente Rosaro and – crossing the stream three times – downhill beneath the bizarrely-shaped rock wall **Sasso Bianco**. Go left to the cemetery and on to **Sassalbo**.

39 Monte Alto, 1904m

The ladders to heaven in Lunigiana

Passo del Cerreto – Passo dell'Ospedalaccio – Monte Alto – Sorgente del Secchia – Passo del Cerreto

Starting point: Passo del Cerreto, 1261m, above Fivizzano.

Access: From Aulla on the well-developed road: 35km (from Reggio nell'Emilia: 75 km).

Walking times: Passo del Cerreto – Passo dell'Ospedalaccio 30 min., to Monte Alto 2 hrs., descent 1½ hrs.; total walking time 4 hrs.

Ascent: Almost 700m.

Grade: Challenging mountain hike with a very steep ascent and a 1-km long, partly exposed ridge crossing (I – II). Very dangerous in the presence of fog or snow. Caution, the descent route often lies under fields of old snow up to the beginning of June!

Refreshment: Bars/ristoranti at the Passo di Cerreto.

Alternative: Passo di Pietra Tagliata – Alpe di Succiso, 2017m, rocky and partly exposed ascent, 45 min.

Map: Carta dei Sentieri e Rifugi No. 14/16 or 15/18, Multigraphic Firenze.

Monte Alto, one of the most precipitous mountains on the northern Tuscan border, possesses an entire spectrum of natural beauty. Its marked ridge route fascinates experienced mountain climbers with tricky climbing spots. From the garden of the **Ristorante »Passo del Cerreto«**, a red-and-white marked trail leads into the wood and then, gently rolling, to the meadow at the **Passo dell'Ospedalaccio**, 1271m. Take a right onto the forestry road to an old French **border stone**, turn to the left there and head up in the direction of »Alpe Succiso«. In meadow

Monte Alto, southeastern ridge.

terrain beneath Monte Alto, a **green post** serves as a waymark: Here, we leave the wide trail and ascend straight on – first to the left, then to the right of a narrow and very steep scree gully.

Finally, we turn right to the **southeastern ridge**, approx. 1800m. Just below the edge, bear left, uphill over boulders and onto a wider, grassy crest. Soon, the ridge becomes narrower again. After several short climbing passages, then over a slab in the right side offering small holds, we reach the upper **ridge tower**, which we ascend on its left side. Cross the sharp edge and head right across an exposed slab in the notch in front of the uppermost peak section. Cross a steep grassy slope to the **summit cairn**. Descend along the narrow trail 673 across the steep grass flank strewn with boulders on the left of the northeastern ridge. Beneath the distinct rock tower, go right across a high rock step and on narrow rock belts to the **Passo di Pietra Tagliata**, 1750m. Go right (no. 671) in bends down to the magical meadow floor surrounding the **Sorgente del Secchia**, approx. 1600m. At the lower end, we reach a fork and head right for a short distance, down to a forest saddle and then downward across the slopes to the turn-off beneath Monte Alto. Go left to the **Passo dell' Ospedalaccio** and the starting point.

The summit above the alpine meadow.

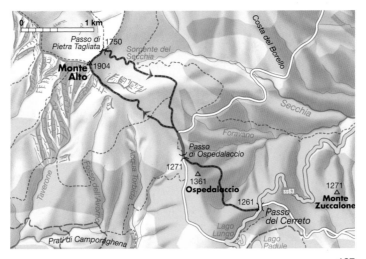

40 Monte Bocco, 1791m

Through the »Park of the Hundred Lakes«

Lago Paduli – Lago Squincio – Monte Malpasso – Monte Bocco – Rifugio Prato Spilla – Lago Verdarolo – Lago Scuro – Lago Paduli

Starting point: 1.5km northeast of the Passo di Lagastrello, 1200m, above the dam of Lago Paduli small car park between a transformer station and a road fork.

Access: From Aulla a short distance in the direction of Pontremoli, then right to the Passo di Lagastrello: 28km (from Parma: 70 km).

Walking times: To Cima Canuti 1½ – 2 hrs., crossing to Monte Bocco 1 hr., descent to Rifugio Prato Spilla 1 hr., return to starting point 1½ hrs.; total walking time 5 – 5½ hrs.

Ascent: All together a good 900m.

Grade: Challenging mountain hike on forest paths and mountain trails with a few steep and exposed sections; sure-footedness and a head for heights are required.

Refreshment: Albergo/Rifugio Prato Spilla (tel. 0521/890194).

Alternative: From Prato Spilla, we recommend a second »lake circuit« via Lago Martini – Monte Sillara, 1861m – Lago Verde – Lago Ballane, 4 – 5 hrs.

Map: Carta dei Sentieri e Rifugi No. 14/16, Multigraphic Firenze.

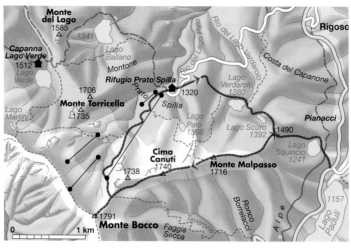

West of the Passo di Lagastrello, Ice-Age glaciers left countless lakes in all sizes and shapes in the Appennine. On this walk you can see a few of them – some from up close, others from the airy Apennine main crest.

The Malpasso, a stony runway over the »Park of the Hundred Lakes«.

Caution, hidden »entry«: Next to the **sign »Comunitá Montana Lunigiana«**, you can make out the triangular **GEA marker** on a telephone pole. This is the start of a red-and-white marked path that leads up towards the mountains through the wood to the old pass route and the smaller dam of **Lago Squincio**, 1241m. Follow marker 703 to the right around the lake and in steep curves to a **forest saddle**, 1490m. Follow marker 00 to the left up the overgrown ridge (difficult, slippery slabs). From the forest border on, we walk on a trouble-free meadow crest to **Monte Malpasso**, 1716m, and **Cima Canuti**, 1740m. We descend via the precipitous grassy crest, over a hilltop, 1730m, and steeply down to a rock precipice. Circumvent the following tower to the right, and the second spike to the left. Cross another grassy hilltop, head across the left slope and over rock steps onto the wide **meadow saddle** above the cableway station (sign). Go straight on over the crest to the cairn on the summit of **Monte Bocco**, 1791m.

Head back to the saddle, then to the left – no markers – down to the cableway station and on the ski track to path 705, on which we walk down to the **Rifugio Prato Spilla**, 1320m. Go right onto the gravel road until it merges with the asphalt road. There, take a right, heading up the steps into the wood, and follow marker 703 across a few boulder-strewn slopes onto a rise. At the following fork, go straight on downhill and then right to **Lago Verdarole**, 1380m. Cross the obstructed drain on the forestry road to the right, then directly afterward, turn left and walk along the forest path to **Lago Scuro**, 1392m. Pass it to the left, walking between boulders, and ascend the curving path through steep forest to the familiar **meadow saddle**, 1490m. The descent follows the ascent route.

41 Monte Marmagna, 1852m

The large cross above Lago Santo

Lagdei – Lago Santo – Monte Marmagna – Monte Braiola – Lagdei

Starting point: Lagdei, 1265m, ski area east of the Passo di Cirone.

Access: From Pontremoli a short distance in the direction of Passo della Cisa, then right onto a narrower road across Passo di Cirone to Cirone; there, right to Lagdei (last short section is a gravel road): 30km (from Parma 55 km).

Walking times: Lagdei – Lago Santo 1 hr., to Monte Marmagna 1 – 1½ hrs., crossing to Monte Braiola 30 min., descent 2 hrs.; total walking time 4½ – 5 hrs.

Ascent: A total of 750m.

Grade: Mountain hike on partially narrow and steep forest paths and meadow trails; one passage requires sure-footedness and a head for heights.

Refreshment: Rifugio Mariotti at Lago Santo.

Alternatives: Side-trip to the rocky Monte Aquiletto, 1788m, 15 min. If you do not wish to cross Monte Braiola, you can descend along a narrow unmarked path from the notch beneath Marmagna and Monte Braiola leading through blueberry bushes to trail no. 729, 30 min. shorter.

Map: Carta dei Sentieri e Rifugi No. 14/16 or 9/13, Multigraphic Firenze.

Parma gets its name neither from cheese nor ham, but rather a river with source on M. Marmagna. The NE side of this mountain, which drops steeply in precipitous rock flanks towards Lunigiana, belongs to the »Park of the 100 Lakes«. The most beautiful of its water holes – as its namesake in the province of Modena – has been considered sacred since primeval times.

A gravel road branches off to the left in front of the car park in **Lagdei**; there is a sign there at the start of the mostly cobblestone path no. 723 a, which leads up through Bosco Corniglio to **Lago Santo** and crosses a few boulder-strewn slopes along the way. Cross a small bridge to the lake outlet and go right along the bank to the **Rifugio Mariotti**, 1507m. Continue on path 719 around the lake, upwards through the wood and past glacier-polished rocks. At the following fork, bear left in the direction of »Passo delle Guadine«, and shortly thereafter, turn right onto path 723 in the direction of »Monte Marmagna«. Walk across the open cirque up onto the meadow crest. Go right, following marker 00 (or directly over the ridge) to the **summit**, 1852m (Ma-

The Rifugio Mariotti.

Green carpet, grey rocks: Monte Aquiletto, around which eagles still circle.

donna and large cross). We descend to the northern secondary summit, then bear left across a very steep grassy slope. We soon reach a **meadow saddle** and head on to **Monte Braiola**, 1821m, then take a right onto trail 00, travelling steeply downhill to **Bocchetta dell'Orsaro**, 1724m. Here, we turn off sharply to the right, and follow marker 729 across the slope and descend into a cirque. Behind a small stone hut, the path forks: Go right in the direction of »Lago Padre, Lago Santo« upward into the wood, over a small rocky notch and down to an almost fully overgrown lake. We continue between boulders to a further overgrown lake. Soon, we reach the ascent route, on which we return to **Rifugio Mariotti**. Shortly after the hut, turn left onto the cobblestone trail 723 (»Diretto«) across the chairlift track and down to **Lagdei**.

Carrara and the Versilia

The Apuane Alps appear to be within grasp from the sandy beach stretching for kilometres and the holiday settlements in Versilia: Here, mountain adventure and bathing pleasure can be had in one and the same day. However, prerequisites are a functioning motor vehicle – and enough confidence, because on these narrow, curvy mountain roads, one lorry after another carts tons of marble blocks into the valley. Hardly any other town has become so synonymous with a product as Carrara, and hardly any other mountain region has been such a victim of economic exploitation as its environs: The marble quarries in the Apuane Alps are already allowed to collect an overall area of 67 km²; in the valley of Colonnata alone, 46 000 tonnes are quarried per month.

Experts estimate the remaining stock of this popular material to amount to 60 billion m³. Even the Romans utilised the natural cracks in the marble by driving wooden stakes into them and pouring water over the stakes – this make the wood swell, which broke the rock open. It was only in the 18th century that blasting was employed, which, in addition to many risks, also produced giant heaps of unusable rubble. Since the late 19th century, marble blocks have been cut out of the mountain with steel cable; this period also saw the birth of the railway line, in the meantime closed down, with its loading stations, tunnels and the famous Ponti di Vara. The use of diamond cable further increased quarried amounts, and today, experiments are already being performed with high-pressure water jets.

The highest marble quarry, however, is found above the valleys merging near Massa and Pietrasanta – all around the 1700-m high Passo della Focolaccia on Monte Tambura and on the 1739-m high Monte Sella. The most

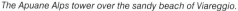

The Apuane Alps tower over the sandy beach of Viareggio.

A ladder to heaven between walls and clouds: Alto di Sella.

unsightly wound in the terrain gapes in the summit ridge of the 1676-m high Monte Corchia. One can find long-since shut-down quarry sites in the middle of the mighty southern precipices of Monte Altissimo, on Monte Sella or in the eastern flank of Monte Sagro, among other locations; they can only be reached on dizzyingly-high transport roads and exposed connection paths. A contrast to this is offered by the hikes on the wooded submountains of Versilia, across isolated hills rising over the reedy Lago di Massaciuccoli, where Giacomo Puccini found inspiration for his most beautiful operas (and enough wind animals to hunt), or through pine groves in the south of the tourist magnet of Viareggio.

PARCO REGIONALE MIGLIARINO, SAN ROSSORE, MASSACIUCCOLI

The 23 000-hectare nature preserve in the coastal forest region between Viareggio and Livorno encompasses sandy beaches, pine woods and the mouths of the rivers Serchio and Arno. The heart of the park consists of the 7-km^2 and only maximally 4-m deep Lago di Massaciuccoli, an overgrown lagoon, and the untouched marshwoods of Tenuta di San Rossore (parts of which can only be visited on certain days and in the presence of a guide). The visitor centre is located in Cascine Vecchie, west of Pisa.

42 To the abandoned Village of Vergheto

Solitude behind the quarries

Colonnata near Carrara – Vergheto

Starting point: Colonnata, 350m.
Access: From Carrara through a wild valley full of marble quarries: 8km (bus connections also).
Walking times: From Colonnata to Vergheto 1¼ hrs., return ¾ hr.; total walking time 2 hrs.
Ascent: 320m.
Grade: Easy walk on forest paths, one short section is steep.

Refreshment: Rifugio Monte Sagro (self-catered huts, tel. 0585/315235). In all bars and alimentari in Colonnata, you can purchase delicious lardo (bacon) cut paper-thin.
Alternative: Worthwhile continuation from Vergheto to Foce Luccica, 1029m, 50 min. there and back.
Map: Carta dei Sentieri e Rifugi No. 101/102, Multigraphic Firenze.

Even in the direct vicinity of the world-famous marble quarries around Carrara, amid droning machines and precariously-manoeuvring transporters, a few oases of solitude have endured. One of them is the abandoned mountain village of Vergheto, which dozes dreamily above Colonnata amid untouched chestnut woods: A lovely hiking destination that offers surprising panoramas of Monte Sagro, the jagged mountain landscape around Monte Tambura, and Monte Altissimo.

Bewitched: An abandoned building in the mountain village of Vergheto.

The marble-quarry village of Colonnata goes back to a Roman slave colony.

Our starting point is the **Piazza Palestro** in front of the Campanile (tower) of **Colonnata**. At its front end, near the Locanda puana, we stroll onto the lane which branches off towards the mountains (street sign »Sackgase«, read »dead-end«, marker 38 on a telephone pole), which leads by a small church. At the last houses, turn left onto a partially cobblestoned trail leading into the wood. After passing a water tank and an old house, turn right, level with the Canale del Vento (wind valley) and to the right over the **bridge**. The trail now leads in turns uphill; soon we see a sign indicating the direction of Vergheto to the left.

Now, we walk higher, in serpentines and over steps through the beautiful chestnut wood – always follow the markers at several forks. We thus arrive at a ridge onto which we turn left and reach the abandoned houses of **Vergheto** (and the closed Rifugio Monte Sagro). The return follows the same route.

43 Monte Sagro, 1748m

High above the sea and marble quarries

Campocecina – Foce di Pianza – Foce di Faggiola – Monte Sagro

Starting point: Campocecina, 1300m, above Carrara.
Access: From Carrara in the direction of Fosdinovo, after 9.5 km, bear right onto the curvy road up toward Campocecina (lorry traffic) and after another 9.5 km, turn left for 3km to the Ristorante Il Belvedere (bus connections from Carrara).
Walking times: Belvedere – Rifugio Carrara – Foce di Pianza 45 min. From there to Monte Sagro 1½ hrs., return route

1¾ hrs.; total walking time 4 hrs.
Ascent: 600m.
Grade: Mountain hike on narrow, partly stony paths; a head for heights and sure-footedness required.
Refreshment: Rifugio Il Belvedere (open year-round, tel. 0585/841973); Rifugio Carrara (18 beds, open year-round, tel. 0585/841972).
Map: Carta dei Sentieri e Rifugi No. 101/102, Multigraphic Firenze.

The western-most of the large Apuane rocky mountains towers over the valleys above Carrara, scarred by over 300 quarries. Even in its peak area, there is drilling and digging, such that this walk can impart varying impressions – from oppressive glimpses of the blinding white stone, to the marvellous summit panorama, which includes the remote Appennine as well as the nearby sea.

Countless machines gnaw at the marble mountains in the hinterland of Carrara.

We begin walking on the cobble-stone path with the marker 173 up to the **Rifugio Carrara**, 1320m. We pass a chapel and come to the large meadow of **Campocecina**, then head left, up to the edge of the wood and around Monte Borla. We make a short descent through a rocky but not difficult slope

Marble summit madonna.

(view to the opposite marble quarries) to the dusty road intersection at **Foce di Pianza**, 1279m (small marble cross). Now, follow marker 172 across the rocky ridge between the road and the quarry, above a tunnel, into a notch and to the right up the ridge. On easily traversed rock steps, we cross the slope up to the hill-like ridge (view down on Colonnata). Head left to a group of trees and to **Foce della Faggiola**, 1464m. Follow the sign »M. Sagro« to the left and on the blue-and-white markered trail through a wide cirque on the northeastern ridge, and along it, to the right to the marble madonna standing under the large **summit cross**.

Descend either along the ascent route or further over the somewhat more difficult but shorter **ridge route**, also markered: This route heads directly toward the marble quarry and snakes further down where the terrain becomes steeper and rockier, down to trail no. 173. Along this route, traverse a basin, go to the edge of the quarries and, above them, to **Foce di Pianza**. From there, you can also return to the starting point via the panoramic asphalt road.

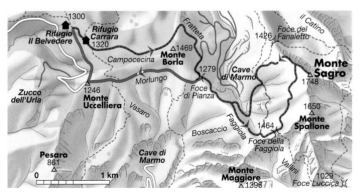

44 Via di Lizza delle Cave Cruze – Via Vandelli

The breathtaking route to the marble quarries in the Stella massif

Resceto – Cave Cruze – Rifugio Conti – Resceto

Starting point: Resceto, 485m.
Access: From Massa in the direction of Forno, after 6.5km right in the direction of Gronda/Resceto: a total of 12 km. Parking at the end of the road above the village.
Walking times: Resceto – Cave Cruze 3 – 3½ hrs., further to Rifugio Conti ½ hr., descent 1½ hrs.; total walking time 5 – 5½ hrs.
Ascent: 1150m.
Grade: Challenging mountain tour with a very steep and partially exposed ascent requiring a head for heights and sure-footedness. Two passages are secured with steel ropes. Be sure to take enough water with you. In the lower portion, there

is shade into the late morning. In the presence of snow or fog, this hike is dangerous; after rainfall, the dry streambed becomes a rushing mountain torrent. The descent is trouble-free.
Refreshment: Rifugio Nello Conti (24 beds; open daily from 20 June to 15 September, otherwise on weekends or staffed for groups per arrangement, tel. 0585/793059 or 0585/315253).
Alternative: From the first fork in Canale dei Piastriccioni, go left directly to the Rifugio (steel ropes); 1 hr.
Map: Carta dei Sentieri e Rifugi No. 101/102, Multigraphic Firenze.

Alpine: the western flank of Alto di Sella, which is crossed by the artfully-constructed »Via di Lizza«.

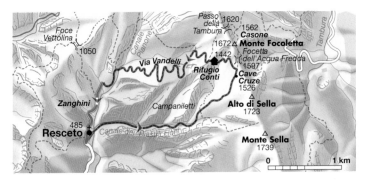

Before construction of the cableway and roads, the marble blocks were brought down to the valleys from the high quarries on perilous tracks lined with walls and stretching for kilometres: Via »lizzatura«, the precious freight was slid down the mountain – similar to a sled – on a construction of rods and logs. This walk follows a »via di lizza«, artfully walled around 1930, through a gorge and up to the high west face of Monte Alto di Sella. It boggles the mind to stand there, grasping the steel rope in front of the most steep section along which workers lowered stone blocks weighing tons and secured by hemp rope (here and there, you can still discover poles used for securing the blocks). We can also only begin to imagine the dangerous work day in Cave Cruze, the quarries active until 1950 amid the flat rock flank. In contrast to Via di Lizza, as steep as a church roof, the countless serpentines of the Via Vandelli lead back to the valley in a gentle descent (see also Walk 35).

From the **church in Resceto**, a hidden stairway leads down to the road that turns off in front of the village on the valley side and leads in front of the houses to the merging of two streams. Follow the markers 160/164/165 to the right across the ford and uphill through the wild valley of the **Canale dei Piastriccioni** (also known as Canale dei Vernacchi). At a walled water tank, go right and along the well-maintained via di lizza, to a destroyed bridge. Before the bridge, go left over the gorge, along a narrow stairway past an old building, and zigzag steeply up to a ridge. Head right into the valley and, walking at times on and at times next to the marble transport road, to a fork, approx. 1000 m: Go right, following the sign in the direction of »Cave Cruze« (no. 165) and over the smoothly-polished stone blocks uphill in the streambed. Soon, the route divides again: Bear left, continuing in the direction of »Cave Cruze« until the path surmounts a very precipitous and grassy, steep step (steel rope). Cross a less steep meadow and a forest ridge to an old building that stands directly beneath the precipices. The via di lizza, now

To the left of the »house on the edge«, a miniature ferrata was established.

once again well-maintained, leads higher across the rocky slope and soon turns to the left – the track is wide, but steeper than it looks from below. At the following forks, remain on the left, lower path. After one last steep stretch and a somewhat narrow passage, we reach the lower quarry of **Cave Cruze**, 1526m. The rocky path leads past a rusty water tank and through the wall to the upper quarry, which has already been »gnawed at« by the edge of the ridge. From the dilapidated **Casa sull' abisso** (house on the cliff edge), the former dwelling of the workers, climb the grassy slope in a few minutes and access the panoramic **Focetta dell' Acqua Fredda**, 1597m. Directly behind the building, on the other hand, the short crossing of a steep but well-stepped rock flank, secured with steel ropes, begins; behind the edge, the trail snakes through a meadow basin down to the **Rifugio Conti**, 1442m.

From the hut, a comfortable path leads in a few minutes between bizarre rock towers to the wide, partly renovated **Via Vandelli**, which leads into the valley in several bends along a comfortable ascent – past a chapel and a wooden resting place. Several locations have signs indicating their elevation. Finally, a bridge spans a deep gorge, after which Route 166 turns off to the left and follows a wide marble transport track down to **Resceto**.

Right: The Rifugio Nello Conti, on the horizon the marble quarries of Carrara.

45 Monte Altissimo, 1589m

Michelangelo's marble mountain

Le Gobbie – Passo degli Uncini – Monte Altissimo – Passo del Vaso Tondo – Cave Fondone – Le Gobbie

Starting point: Ristorante Le Gobbie, 1037m, east of the street tunnel between Rifugio Città di Massa and Arni.
Access: From Massa in the direction of Castelnuovo di Garfagnana via Antona, past the Rifugio Città di Massa: 17 km.
Walking times: Le Gobbie – Passo degli Uncini 1¼ hrs., summit ascent 45 min., descent to starting point 1½ – 2 hrs.; total walking time 3½ – 4 hrs.
Ascent: A total of 650m.

Grade: Challenging mountain hike with exposed slope crossings and airy ridge crossing (I); A head for heights and sure-footedness necessary! Very dangerous in the presence of precipitation or snow!
Refreshment: Bar/Ristorante Le Gobbie; Rifugio Città di Massa (150 beds; open daily from May to September, otherwise only on weekends, tel. 0585/319923).
Map: Carta dei Sentieri e Rifugi No. 101/102, Multigraphic Firenze.

Monte Altissimo is by far not the highest peak in Versilia. However, seen from the ocean, it really does appear to have a monumental size: This is due to its 700-m high south face, stretching for kilometres, in which none other than Michelangelo had the first marble quarries constructed. The master artist probably never crossed its sharp summit ridge – today, its spectacular panorama is still only reserved for experienced mountain climbers.

From the car park at the **Ristorante Le Gobbie**, we hike – following the signs to »Monte Altissimo« and the red-and-white marker 33 – uphill alongside the Canale di Grotta Giancona. Soon, turn left, cross an old marble transport road to an **intersecting road**. Head straight on along path no. 41 up to the **Passo d' Angiola** (Foce del Frate), 1327m. There, turn left, pass under

Two towers: Monte Altissimo and the Campanile of the church of Arni.

Monte Altissimo and its ridges, as seen from Pania delle Croce.

the ridge edge into a forest saddle and further to the **Passo degli Uncini**, 1380m. Cross the crest briefly, then head left on very narrow rock steps up across the **steep slope**. In the wood once again, we then to the right and ascend very steeply to the **ridge**. On the ridge, bear left and, at times on and at times alongside the sharp ridge edge, walk to the small summit cross.

Descend along the more simple path 143 which, in its lower section is even walled: First we continue on the ridge, then head left downhill and beneath the ridge edge to **Passo del Vaso Tondo**, 1440m. Further along, old war shelters and marble quarries can be seen. After a small **notch**, turn sharply

to the left and walk along path 142 to **Cave Fondone**. At a transformer station, bear right to a gravel road which leads down to the quarry. After a right-hand curve (next to an old, cave-like quarry), head sharply down to the left and following the path up and down, past further quarries. Finally, **ascent route** no. 33 intersects with our path, onto which we turn right and head back down to the starting point.

46 Forest Trails to the Foce di Mosceta

Hiking bliss, even without a summit

Passo di Croce – Passo di Fociomboli – Puntato – Rifugio del Freo – Passo di Croce

Starting point: Passo di Croce, 1160m, above Levigliani.

Access: From Serravezza in the direction of Castelnuovo di Garfagnana; after approx. 13km (beyond Levigliani) go right on the 5-km long asphalt road up to the top of the pass (lorry traffic).

Walking times: Passo di Croce – Puntato 1½ hrs., to the Rifugio del Freo 1½ hrs., crossing to Passo di Croce 1½ hrs.; total walking time 4½ hrs.

Ascent: 550m.

Grade: Easy walk on trouble-free forest trails that are not always well-marked.

Refreshment: Rifugio Giuseppe del Freo – Pietrapana (31 beds; open daily from mid-June to mid-September, otherwise staffed on most weekends, open overnight room, tel. 0584/778007).

Alternatives: From the Foce di Mosceta on a steep trail (126) to the Pania della Croce, 2 hrs. (see also Walk 29). Or, from the Rifugio del Freo to Monte Corchia, 1½ hrs.

Map: Carta dei Sentieri e Rifugi No. 101/102, Multigraphic Firenze.

An extended forest hike can make you hungry: a picnic in front of one of the shepherds' houses in Puntato.

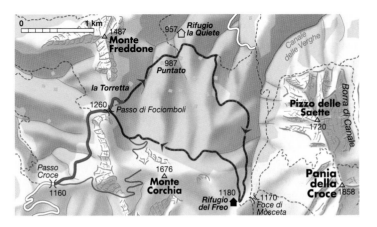

This circuit tour combines interesting nature and cultural history points beneath the 1676-m high Monte Corchia, the mountain with the most caves in the Apuane Alps. In the summit area, marble is quarried – but its old shepherds' settlements are abandoned, the charcoal kilns extinguished.

From the fork beyond **Passo di Croce**, we follow the left-hand, lower road, partially paved and partially gravel, which crosses up beneath the Dolomite-like rock walls of Monte Corchia and to the **Passo di Fociomboli**, 1260m. There, turn left and follow the red-and-white marker 11 downhill. After passing two stone huts, turn sharply to the left onto a narrower path to the outlet of the **Torbiera di Fociomboli**, a bog which developed from a lake. Head down next to the stream, cross the water at a spring water chamber and follow the curves in the path to the shepherds' houses of **Puntato**, 987m, which are situated across from Monte Freddone. Take a right at the church, walk downhill under chestnut trees and straight across the wooded slope to a ridge. Ascend the ridge to the right (barely discernible colour marker), then head left past dilapidated buildings. Soon a yellow-markered, amost completely preserved **cobblestone path** intersects, onto which we turn left and follow it to another tumbledown house. The path gently rises and falls to **Tana dell' Omo Selvatico**, a large doline, and into a meadow valley beneath Pania della Croce. To the west, across from **Foce di Mosceta**, is the **Rifugio del Freo**, 1180m. Beyond it to the right, we find trail 129, which leads in the direction of »Ficiomboli« uphill through a coniferous wood. From a clear slope, the view stretches to Monte Matanna. In the wood, walk steeply up to a **saddle**, then, in steady rises and falls, to a fork: Go straight on, past a dilapidated hut and down to a gravel road. Take the gravel road across the nearby **Passo di Fociomboli** back to the starting point.

47 Monte Forato, 1223 m

A challenging climb to the rock arch

Stazzema – Foce di Petrosciana – Via Ferrata Salvadori – Monte Forato

Starting point: Above Stazzema, 443m.
Access: From Pietrasanta via Serravezza; in the left-hand curve before Stazzema, straight on (sign »Rifugio Forte dei Marmi«) and around two more curves to the turn-off of the hiking paths: 19 km. On workdays, bus connections to Stazzema, from there on foot 30 min.
Walking times: Stazzema – Foce di Petrosciana 1½ hrs., to Monte Forato 1 hr., descent 2 hrs.; total walking time 4½ hrs.
Ascent: 700m.
Grade: Challenging mountain hike on forest paths and an exposed fixed rope route (only accessible with fixed-rope equipment and experience in such routes), which can also be circumvented.
Refreshment: Albergo Procinto in Stazzema.
Alternatives: The fixed rope route can be circumvented by continuing on the forest path under the large rocky rise (one portion is indistinct). A longer hike: Ascending the village Cardoso, descent through the rock arch and via Collemezzana, 5 – 6 hrs.
Map: Carta dei Sentieri e Rifugi No. 101/102, Multigraphic Firenze.

On Monte Forato, Mother Nature shows her whimsical side: A 26-m high and 32-m wide breakthrough gapes open between both peaks. The rock arch over Cardoso is impressive, and at certain points along the Serchio valley – such as Fornovolasco – it presents another spectacle: In that location, on a few evenings in October, November and March, you can observe the sun go down directly behind the opening.

We begin at the fork above **Serravezza** (sign »M. Forato«) and follow marker 5/6 to the first of several stone chapels that line our route. At the following fork, bear left, following marker 6 uphill, on a partially cobblestoned path, past two buildings (do not turn right), and beneath the rock precipices of Monte Procinto up to Casa Aglieta. Walk on level ground to a fork: Head straight on to **Fonte Moscoso**, 830m, and at the following branch, to the right.

On the Salvatori fixed rope route.

After path 109 merges, we reach another stone chapel: Turn right and ascend for a brief time to the **Foce di Petrosciana**, 961m. This spot marks the beginning of the **Sentiero Renato Salvatori**, established in 1978, which ascends over a partially stone ridge (steel rope) to a vertical rock rise. We

climb over it with the aid of steel ropes and chains. Via a ladder, we reach the exposed ridge edge, which we cross along the ropes. Finally, we head over a wooded saddle and another rise to the wooded **main summit**, 1229m.

Go right, down to the **rock arch** and a brief distance to the cross on the open **northern summit**, 1209m (magnificent view of the massif of Panie with the facial features of the »Uomo morto«).

The return route follows the path which leads to the left into the forest above the rock arch, and which crosses down to the entry of the fixed rope route beneath the ridge edge (it is indistinct in one spot). Continue on the ascent path to the **Foce di Petrosciana** and back to the starting point.

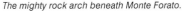

The mighty rock arch beneath Monte Forato.

48 Monte Nona, 1279m

Wild walls, wide view

Stazzema – Rifugio Forte dei Marmi – Monte Nona – Albergo Alto Matanna – Foce delle Porchette – Stazzema

Starting point: As in Walk 47.
Access: As in 47.
Walking times: To the Rifugio Forte dei Marmi 1¼ hrs., to Monte Nona 1¼ hrs., return via Alto Matanna 2½ hrs.; total walking time 5 hrs.
Ascent: A total of 950m.
Grade: Mountain hike on forest paths and rocky trails, some of which require a head for heights.
Refreshment: Albergo Procinto in Stazzema; Rifugio Forte dei Marmi (open daily from mid-June to mid-September, otherwise on most weekends, tel. 05 84/777051); bar and sale of local specialities in the Albergo Alto Matanna (tel. 05 84/776005).
Alternative: Via Ferrata (Sentiero Aristide Bruni) to Monte Procinto, 1039m (only with fixed-rope equipment), 1½ hrs. there and back. Callare di Matanna – Monte Matanna, 1317m, 45 min.
Map: Carta dei Sentieri e Rifugi No. 101/102, Multigraphic Firenze.

The Monte Procinto.

The well-visited panoramic mountain over Versilia shows a Janus face: Steep grassy slopes on the east side and, in the west, a vertical wall before which the bizarre block of rock of Monte Procinto rears up: It was »tamed« as early as 1893 with ladders, steel ropes and 265 constructed steps.

As in Walk 47, follow the **sign** »M. Forato« on path 5/6 to the nearby fork, and turn right there (No. 5) uphill through the wooded slopes. After a well, turn right beneath rocks to the next fork, where we head right and soon reach the **Rifugio Forte dei Marmi** on Alpe della Grotta, 868m. Walk back and to the right up over a rocky passage (steel rope).

At the following fork, head straight on, following marker 5 (to the left, you come to the fixed rope route onto Monte Procinto) and turn right beneath the wall of Monte Nona.

From Monte Nona, the view stretches down to Stazzema and Monte Procinto.

Pass a large **rock arch** and walk over exposed rock steps to **Callare di Matanna**, 1139m (cross, power lines). Turn sharply to the left and cross the grassy southern ridge (blue markers, small rock steps) to the metal cross on **Monte Nona**, 1279m. Go back to the notch, but now turn left down to the

Albergo Alto Matanna, 1037m. At a gate beyond the house, path no. 109 branches off to the left, which crosses the grassy slopes of Monte Nona and snakes down through the wood to **Foce delle Porchette**, 982m. From the stone chapel, the path leads straight on over the ridge, then left through a rocky gorge and beneath the wall of Monte Croce. In the wood, turn sharply to the left and then continue to follow Marker 6 to the **Fonte Moscoso**, 830m (there is also a direct descent from Foce delle Porchette on path no. 8). Go straight ahead to Casa Aglieta and turn right beneath Monte Procinto in the direction of »Stazzema« back down to the starting point.

49 Through Macchia Lucchese near Viareggio

Forest and beach adventure for trailblazers

Instructive nature trail – lagoon – sandy beach and back

Starting point: Viareggio, Pizzeria La Lecciona in Viale dei Tigli (across from Villa Borbone), situated approximately equidistant between the harbour and Torre del Lago.
Access: From the harbour in Viareggio in the direction of Torre del Lago: 3 km. Also accessible by bus or (rental) bicycle.
Walking time: 2 hrs.
Ascent: Negligible.
Grade: Forest walk on sand roads and a waymarked path that is partially obstructed by forestry work; difficult orientation in a few spots.
Refreshment: At the starting point, in Via-

reggio and Torre del Lago.
Alternative: The walk can be extended as desired on several forest roads and the path along the dunes.
Map: Information board with route sketches at the start of the instructive nature trail; town map of Viareggio available in the tourist offices (e.g. at Piazza d'Azeglio). Carta della Natura e degli Ambiti Territoriali Parco Regionale Migliarino / San Rossore / Massaciuccoli (1:33.000), S.E.L.C.A. Firenze (available in the Cascine Vecchie Visitor Centre near Pisa or in the LIPU Museum in Massaciuccoli, see Walk 50).

Between Versilia and Livorno, around the mouths of the Serchio and Arno rivers, is one of the most extensive coastal forests in Southern Europe. A 23,000-hectare regional park protects this natural wonder, which also encompasses the remains of a giant lagoon, the Lago di Massaciuccoli. The most precious areas near Pisa may only be accessed in the context of a guided tour. The Macchia Lucchese and its undeveloped sandy beach, on the other hand, belong to the nearby recreational area around Viareggio, which is best explored along an instructional nature trail set up by the WWF.

We enter the **Pineta dei Levante** on the sand road branching off toward the ocean next to the pizzeria (sign »Parco Naturale Macchia Lucchese«). Soon, a sign indicates the be-

ginning of the »**Percorso natura**« to the right. Directly afterward, we turn to the left, onto a narrower path, walk across a canal and follow the other arrows and plant identification signs, crossing a forestry road in the process. After two wooden walkways, the way is blocked by fallen trees: We can circumvent that spot on the right; then, we follow a wider road to the left, until the hidden sign »Olivella« indicates the further route through the wood on the right. Thus, we reach the second information board with route sketches and the wider path leading along the beach. Behind it, we

Bindweed blooms in the dunes.

climb over wood steps onto the **dune wall**, beyond which a small lagoon with birdwatching stations is located. From there, it is not far to the undeveloped **sandy beach**. From the information board, you can walk back onto the instructional nature trail, or follow the sand path a bit in the direction of Marina di Torre del Lago and return to the starting point along the sand road branching off to the left.

Two worlds: The Apuane Alps above the untouched stretch of beach.

50 The Hills above the Lago di Massaciuccoli

Ocean view and other surprises

Massaciuccoli – Aquilata – Villa Hernandez – Compignano and back

Starting point: Massaciuccoli, LIPU Oasi.
Access: From Viareggio in the direction of Lucca to Quiesta near Massarosa, there, turn off toward Massaciuccoli and turn right in the village to the LIPU Oasi on Lago di Massaciuccoli: 14km (from Lucca: 17 km). Boat connections from Torre del Lago (Villa Puccini) near Viareggio.
Walking times: Lago di Massaciuccoli – Roman Villa 30 min., to Compignano 2 hrs., return route 2 hrs., total walking time 4½ hrs.
Ascent: 400m.
Grade: Easy hike on winding forest trails,

in between overgrown sections and short sections of street. Despite the markers, orientation is not easy in all areas.
Refreshment: Bar and pizzerias in Massaciuccoli.
Alternative: From the LIPU Oasi on the walkway into the reedy area at the lake shore (birdwatching stations), 30 min. there and back.
Map: Carta della Natura e degli Ambiti Territoriali Parco Regionale Migliarino/San Rossore/Massaciuccoli (on a scale of 1 : 33,000), S.E.L.C.A. Firenze (available in the LIPU Museum in Massaciuccoli).

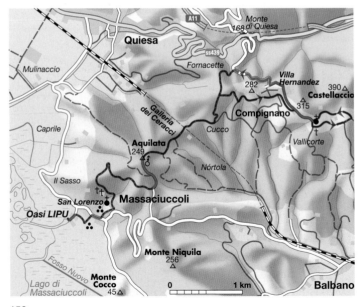

The prettiest spot to look out over Lago di Massaciuccu li is the forecourt of the church in the town of the same name, on its eastern shore – directly over the ruins of a Roman villa, including thermal baths from the 2nd and 3rd century. Behind them, the southernmost foothills of the Apuane Alps emerge – peaceful wooded hills which repeatedly allow surprising panoramas out to Pisa and Lucca.

At an information board next to the **LIPU Oasi** at the lake shore (landing-pier), the red markers of »**Percorso 2**« begin, which initially leads us along Via del Porto. After the hotel, turn right onto Via delle Redole. At the start of the gravel road, turn left onto a trail leading to a **Roman excavation site** and turn right on the main road for a short distance. On the other side, there is an information board next to a fork: There, we walk up a few steps between olive trees, past the ruins of the **Roman villa**, and left to the **church of San Lorenzo**, 153m.

Continue somewhat downhill, on the gravel road, passing above the **cemetery** and heading onto a forest ridge. Here, head left on a narrow, steep trail past a house (beware of dog!) and to the right near an old steel scaffolding. Walk through overgrown brush, then right, downhill to an old house and along the forestry road, gently rising and falling (pretty view of the lake) to the asphalt road (information board). Turn sharply left onto this road and walk upwards to a **rest area**, then continue left, then left on a

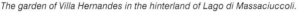

The garden of Villa Hernandes in the hinterland of Lago di Massaciuccoli.

A wobbly footbridge leads to the birdwatching stations in the reed belt.

gravel road to the radio towers on the hill of **Aquilata**, 249m. Head right downhill along the forest trail and – always keeping right – around the forest ridge to a forestry track which runs along a fence and leads to a meadow with two benches. Turn right here, passing under the power lines, and bear left uphill at the fork. Walk along the overgrown forest trail to a **gate** which we climb over, then follow the path branching off to the right into an olive grove. Between two fences, we fight our way though the high »fern jungle« uphill until we reach more open terrain down to the right. There, bear left, heading toward the large **Villa Hernandez**. After the historical cobblestone path of Acciottolato merges, we pass beneath the garden of the Villa, until we reach an asphalt road at a house. Head right onto this road to a rest area and to the nearby **church of San Frediano** in **Compignano**, 290m. Turn right onto the gravel road to the **cemetery**, and turn left before the cemetery and head into the wood. After the benches, turn left and walk along a trail over the hill, 350m (view of the Lucca basin). Walk across the meadow and past a group of oak trees, and shortly thereafter, veer to the left onto a gravel road and past a house. At the next house, turn left onto the asphalt road and back down to the **San Frediano church**. Back to the **Villa Hernandez**, pass it on the right and walk beneath the neighbouring **Villa Baldini** in curves downhill until the gravel Via del Cucco next to an information board leads to the left into the wood. Where the asphalt surface begins, we turn left through an opening in a fence to the familiar **gate**, and from there, head right, back along the access route. From the first rest area on, you can also continue on the asphalt road: At a madonna chapel, turn right and head down to **Massaciuccoli** in wide curves.

Villa with a lake view: The Roman ruins above Lago di Massaciuccoli.

Index